I0462317

BOOKKEEPING

Comprehensive Beginners' Guide to Learning the Simple and Effective Methods of Bookkeeping

TABLE OF CONTENTS

Introduction

Whether you are just starting your business or have had your business for years, it is important to know bookkeeping.

Bookkeeping has been around for centuries. However, it has evolved over time to help your business keep track of your finances better.

Bookkeeping covers a long list of aspects that help the business owner make decisions about the company. To better understand bookkeeping, my goal is to help you get a good feel for knowing how to read the financial reports, the basics of bookkeeping, employees, understanding the balance sheet and income statement, and so much more.

Come along with me as we explore the world of bookkeeping and help you, the business owner, understand how to make sense out of bookkeeping.

As an added bonus, I have included a section for your business taxes. I also included a step-by-step process of preparing W-2 forms and the information that is needed for those. You will soon find out that there is more to it than just providing the information and typing it up on the W-2 form.

Keep reading, and you will see what it takes to get on the same page as your bookkeeper. I always said, "It is not the business owner that runs the business. It is the business owner teamed up with the bookkeeper that truly runs the business."

Running a business can be fun and rewarding. However, if you do not have the basic knowledge of the fundamental financial skills needed, it can prove to be stressful as well.

Throughout this book, you will learn the basics of bookkeeping and finding the right bookkeeper for you. As you go through it, you will also learn about the ledgers and journals. It is important that you know where your money is at all times. I also take the time to talk to you about hiring employees. Let's face it—if your business is going to grow above a certain level, you will eventually need to hire someone to work with you.

There is also a lot of software available to help you with all your bookkeeping needs, although not all accounting software is right for your business. We will take a look at a few of the top-rated applications and give you both the good and the bad of each one.

Don't forget: you also need to understand those scary financial statements. That's why we will take a look at the four main financial statements and break them down for you so that you can easily read and understand each one.

It does not matter if you have been in business for a couple of years or are just starting; you will be filing taxes at the end of the year. This is a lot of work, and your bookkeeper can help you get prepared.

Did you know that as a business owner, you can deduct a lot of your expenses? I included that as well. It is only a small list, and with a little research, you could probably find more.

Finally, I also included, in detail, how to go about preparing, distributing, and filing the employees' W-2s.

So come along with me as we take this glorious adventure into bookkeeping for small businesses and give you the power to understand your business's financial health.

What Is Bookkeeping?

Simply put, bookkeeping is the process of recording a business's financial transactions, such as its sales, purchases, payments, and receipts, on a daily basis.

These records must be accurate and up-to-date and should be able to provide a clear picture of the performance of the business after a specific period.

How Bookkeeping Works

Whenever any individual or corporate body buys anything from you or sells anything to you, you have to record the exact details of the transaction and keep the documents used to transact the business as backup evidence.

You would then use the individual records you have made to set up financial statements at the end of a period, which could be daily, weekly, monthly, or yearly.

Why Bookkeeping?

Bookkeeping may involve historical records, but these records are very vital to the success of any business.

Here are some of the very important reasons for bookkeeping:

- Bookkeeping provides a true and accurate picture of the business. To know how your business is performing, whether you are making gains or losses, growing or dwindling, the only way you can know these is if you keep accurate records.

- There is the issue of taxes; you have to be able to know just how much taxes you need to pay at the end of every year.

- It helps you easily forecast and create plans for your business. By looking at your bookkeeping records, you can easily say, "We always sell 500 units of X product every December, so this year, we should work on increasing our sales to XX units."

- If you have investors or third parties such as shareholders or partners who would be interested in the performance of your business, well-kept books are the only way you can show them how your business is really doing.

- Through bookkeeping, you can also easily figure out thefts, dishonesty, or poor performances if you have employees or people running your business for you.

- Another benefit you can derive from adequate business bookkeeping is that you can use your financial statements as proofs of business performance if you need to secure loans for your business.

- Bookkeeping shall also help you monitor your business expenses in relation to income.

With that understanding on the importance of bookkeeping, let's now move on to understanding some key terms that are used in bookkeeping and accounting in general before we can get to the point of discussing how to go about bookkeeping.

Accounting System

Definition of Important Accounting Terms

To understand bookkeeping, you need to understand some very important accounting terms, most of which we will cover below:

Assets: Your assets are any resources or things of value owned by your business whose utility is not limited to a single accounting period and whose value can be reasonably estimated.

An example of an asset is a building; the building is relevant to your business for more than one year, and you can easily estimate the financial value of the building. On the other hand, your electricity bill for last month does not count as an asset because the value is only limited to a specific period.

Assets can be tangible like buildings and equipment, or intangible things like intellectual properties and trademarks.

Equity: Equity refers to the ownership interest (stock or contributions) in a business or in a personal asset. For instance, if your home is worth $200,000 and you still have a mortgage loan of $80,000, it means you have a $120,000 equity on the house, or if you and your partner each contribute $50,000 to start a business worth $100,000, it means you both have 50% equity in the business.

Liability: Liabilities refer to your business obligations. You can also see it as what your business owes to other people. It could be money you borrowed, responsibilities you owe to others, or a transaction that has already occurred but is yet to be paid for.

Debit (dr.) and credit (cr.): In accounting, credit is anything that reduces your assets or expenses account or increases your liability or equity account.

On the other hand, debit is any transaction that decreases your liability or equity account or increases your assets or expenses account.

In double entry bookkeeping (more on that later), every transaction affects two accounts; one account gains something while the other account loses something. The account that loses value is credited while the one that gains value is debited.

Below is an example of the use of debit and credit in accounting:

Your business, XYZ Limited buys equipment for $10,000 on credit. This means that your equipment and machinery (assets) has an addition to it, so you debit that account. Nevertheless, since you have not paid for the equipment, you are still indebted. This means your business liability account has increased so what you would do is to credit your accounts payable (liability) account to reflect this increase.

See the illustration below:

Debit

Credit

Equipment and machinery account (fixed assets)

$10,000

Accounts payable

$10,000

Let's take another example category. Assuming XYZ Ltd. sells a product to a customer for $500, it means that the business earns revenue of $500 and that there is an increase in cash (assets) of $500, so you debit the asset account and credit the revenue account.

Debit

Credit

Cash

$500

Revenue

$500

We shall deeply discuss debits and credits in section 3. In the meantime, here is a basic rule for crediting and debiting accounts.

- Increase in asset–debit

- Increase in expenses–debit

- Decrease in liability (when you finally make payments from money you owe)–debit

- Decrease in equity–debit

- Increase in liability (when you incur fresh debts or add to the existing ones)–credit

- Increase in equity–credit

- Decrease in assets–credit

- Decrease in expenses–credit

Revenue/income: In accounting, revenue and income often have interchangeable meaning and uses. Revenue refers to all monies earned by your business regardless of whether they have been collected at the time of reporting or otherwise.

Receipts: Receipts refer to the portion of revenue in business transactions already paid up.

Profits: In accounting, your profit refers to what remains of your revenue/income after you deducting all business expenses. Profits come in two categories: net profits and gross profits.

Gross profits equal your total sales less the costs of goods sold (such as the cost of raw materials, production, delivery costs, etc.) while net profit equals your gross profit less other business expenses not directly related to sales of goods such as taxes, costs of depreciation, and interests.

Losses: Losses refer to any reduction in net income or assets of your business.

With that understanding of the basic terms, let's now learn about some basic principles of accounting.

Choosing Your Accounting System

When choosing your accounting system, you need to make two major decisions:

1. Cash versus accrual-based accounting

2. Double-entry versus single-entry bookkeeping

1: Cash versus Accrual-Based Accounting

There are two different methods used to record accounting transactions: the cash-based method and the accrual-based method. Choose the most suitable one for your business depending on the size of the business.

Cash-Based Accounting

Under this accounting system, you only record revenue/income and expenses whenever there is an actual exchange of cash. You only record expenses and purchases when you have paid cash for them and income when a customer has paid for the goods/services.

For instance, if Mr. A buys a product or receives a service from you in January but does not pay for it until May, you would have to wait until May when Mr. A pays for it before you record the transactions.

Benefits of Cash-Based Accounting

Using the cash-based system of accounting has some advantages:

- Very simple and uncomplicated such that you can easily handle your bookkeeping with zero accounting knowledge/experience.

- You don't need complex software or accounting records; oftentimes, all you need is your check booklet.

Naturally, everything that has an upside also has a downside:

Downsides of Cash-Based Accounting

Cash-based accounting is not always advisable to use because it provides insufficient records and does not really provide a true and clear picture of what is really going on in the business. For instance, you could erroneously report that your business made losses in January because you were yet to receive payments for the products/services sold.

Cash-based accounting also focuses on revenues and expenses alone and ignores other aspects of the business such as assets, inventory, liabilities, equity, and so on.

It also does not conform to the generally accepted accounting principles (GAP) or international financial reporting standards (IFRS).

Which Types of Businesses can Use Cash-Based Accounting System?

Legally, only a few businesses have the green light to use the cash-based system of accounting. You can use cash-based accounting if your business falls within any of the following categories:

- Sole proprietorship with annual average gross receipts of less than $1,000,000

- S-Corporation with annual average gross receipts of less than $1,000,000

- C-Corporation with annual average gross receipts of less than $5,000,000

- A company not publicly traded or not under any obligation to make full disclosure to the IRS

- Family-owned farms with annual gross receipts of less than $25,000,000

Accrual-Based Accounting

Under the accrual-based accounting system, you record transactions when earnings are made and expenses are incurred, not when they are paid for.

In this case, dollar bills or checks do not have to exchange hands before you record such transactions; every time a transaction occurs, you have to record it in your books.

For example, let's assume YXL Ltd. hires you to repair some of its equipment in January and you charge them $5,000 for this service. However, YXL Ltd. does not issue a check immediately but promises to discuss it with the financial accountant and then get back to you. This system of accounting requires that you record this transaction in your accounts receivable books as soon as you complete the job whether YXL makes payments for it or not.

There are two major account items you have to record when using the accrual method of accounting:

Accounts receivable: Account receivable would include all the monies owed to your business not paid.

In this example, as soon as you send out your invoice for the sales of a product or service, you record the value in your accounts receivable ledger.

This account helps you track everything owed to your business.

Accounts payable: Account payable is the exact opposite of accounts receivable. Here, you record all the monies your business owes to other people.

As soon as you receive an invoice or make a commitment to the other party, you have to record the transaction in your account payable book so you can track what your business owes to other people.

Definitions

Bookkeeping

Bookkeeping is the process of recording business transactions. Bookkeeping establishes the foundation for accounting.

Accounting

Accounting is the process of preparing financial statements by summarizing the business transactions recorded through bookkeeping. Accounting also includes analyzing and reporting financial information in a manner that facilitates business decision making.

Revenues

Revenues are all monies earned by a business in any given period of time. Revenues can be derived from sales of goods, sales of services, interest, and any miscellaneous sources.

However, capital deposits are not revenues. Also, monies from loans are not to be considered as revenues either.

Expenses

Expenses are all monies spent by a business. Operating expenses are expenses directly related to the normal operation of a business, which include rents, salaries, supplies, etc. Operating expenses tend to be recurring.

Nonoperating expenses are expenses not related to the normal operation of a business. As such, nonoperating expenses are usually not recurring. One example of nonoperating expenses would be the settlement cost of a lawsuit.

Profits

After ascertaining the total amount of revenues and the total amount of expenses, *profit*[1] can be calculated via a profit equation as follows:

Profit = Revenues - Expenses

The main goal of many businesses is to increase profits. It is clear from the profit equation that profit can be increased by increasing revenues and/or reducing expenses.

Deductible Expenses

Under the Internal Revenue Code, certain business expenses (both operating and nonoperating expenses) are considered as tax *deductible expenses*. In order to minimize income tax payments, a business owner should become familiar with the tax treatment of various deductible expenses.

Many business expenses are deductible in their entirety in the fiscal year[2] in which they are incurred, and some examples of such business expenses are as follows:

Advertising parking fees

Bad debts postage

Bank charges printing

Commissions professional services

Contract services profit-sharing plans

Donations rent

Dues repairs

Educational fees/materials salaries

Food and entertainment subscriptions

Insurance taxes

Legal fees telephone

License fees tools

Loan interest uniforms

Office equipment utility bills

Office supplies vehicle expenses

Depreciable Assets

Instead of the deductible in their entirety in the year in which they are incurred, the expenses on certain business assets, such as business properties, production machinery, office furniture, vehicles, etc., need to be deducted over multiple years. This group of assets is known as *depreciable assets*. The method for deducting the costs of depreciable assets over multiple years is known as *depreciation*.

Section 179 Deduction

Under § 179 of the Internal Revenue Code, when a depreciable asset is qualified as a *qualifying property*, a business is allowed to treat all or part of the cost of the depreciable asset as an expense completely deductible in the year in which it is incurred, instead of over multiple years.

Assets, Liabilities, and Equity

The financial condition of a business can be expressed by the relationship of *assets* to *liabilities* and *owner's equity*.

Assets are all properties owned by a business. Assets include current assets and long-term assets. Current assets are items that can be converted into cash within one year or less, such as cash-in-bank and account receivable. Long-term assets are any assets that are not considered as current assets, such as property and equipment.

Liabilities are all debts the business currently has outstanding to creditors. Liabilities include current liabilities and long-term liabilities. Current liabilities are debts that need to be paid off within one year or less, such as account payable. Long-term liabilities are any liabilities that are not considered as current liabilities.

Owner's equity is the interest of an owner in the business. Owner's equity may include capital and retained earnings.

Accounting Equation

Assets, liabilities and owner's equity are related to each other via a fundamental equation known as the *accounting equation*. The accounting equation states that, without exceptions, the following relationship must always be true:

Assets = Liabilities + Owner's Equity

According to the accounting equation, a business is assumed to possess its assets subject to the rights of its creditors and owners.

For example, when a business owns assets of $200,000, owes creditors $120,000, and owes the business owner $80,000, the accounting equation looks like this:

$$200,000 = 120,000 + 80,000$$

Assets Liabilities Owner's Equity

After a period of time, when the business pays off $15,000 of the debt, the liabilities are reduced by $15,000. If the assets are not changed, the owner's equity is increased by $15,000, and the accounting equation becomes this:

$$200,000 = 105,000 + 95,000$$

Assets Liabilities Owner's Equity

Transaction

A *transaction* is any business event that alters the amount of assets, liabilities, and/or owner's equity.

Journalizing

Every transaction must be recorded as an entry in a journal in chronological order, and the process is called *journalizing*.

Bookkeeping Basics

B efore we get started on breaking down bookkeeping, we need to look at some of the basics. I want you to have the ability to read your financial records and understand them. This will allow you to know the financial aspect of your business. In turn, it will allow you to make good decisions that can increase the growth of your business.

Double-Entry Method

Bookkeeping uses a method called the double-entry bookkeeping. This means that for every entry, there is at least one debit and one credit.

I want you to remember this equation:

- Assets = Liabilities + Equity

This is the basic formula for the double-entry method and will come into play with every transaction you make.

Source Documents

Every transaction made will have a source document. Source documents could be anything from a contract to a gas receipt. If you spent the business's money, then you will need some form of proof of how much you spent. These are the source documents.

These documents will give us all the information you will need to record it in the books. This includes referencing the source documents. Some software will allow you to attach the scanned file to the transaction so that at any time you can bring up the source document.

End-of-Period Procedures

End-of-period procedures relate to not only quarters. Even though all the transactions have been recorded throughout the months or year, they still are not ready for preparing the financial reports.

To ensure that you have your books accurate for preparing the financial reports, you need to consider that there are procedures that need to happen at least at month-end, year-end, and the end of payroll year.

The following outline will show, as a guideline, what should be done during each time.

1.   Month-end procedures

- Run the company/business data auditor.

- Reconcile your bank accounts.

- Review reports.

- Send customer statements.

- Record depreciation.

- Pay payroll taxes.

- Lock periods.

2.   Year-end procedures (to prepare for the new fiscal year)

- Complete month-end tasks.

- Perform an inventory count.

- Provide information to your accountant.

- Enter end-of-year adjustments.

- Back up your company/business file.

- Start the new fiscal year.

- Optimize and verify your company/business file.

3.   End-of-payroll year (to prepare for the new fiscal year). Note: Do not update tax tables.

- Run your last payroll.

- Optimize and verify your company/business file.

- Back up your company/business file.

- Start a new payroll year.

- Install product updates.

- Run your first payroll.

- Restore your backup.

- Print year-end payroll forms.

- Print Vendor 1099 statements.

- Print payroll reports.

Compile the Adjusted Trial Balance

Making these adjustments are very important. When looking at which adjustments need to be made first, you need to gather and compile a spreadsheet that will allow for your trial balance entries as well as the adjustments.

Keep in mind that these adjustments are for correcting errors in the initial trial balance so that everything will come to balance. This form for the adjustments is an internal form but will be used for helping compile the financial statements. Now that automated systems like Xero and QuickBooks are used, the trial balance worksheet is not often practiced. However, it is still a good source document. This is, in part, due to the automated systems creating the reports for you.

Here is an example of what the worksheet may look like:

Frank's Financials

Trial Balance

August 31, 20XX

Unadjusted

Trial Balance Adjusted

Entries   Adjusted

Trial Balance

Cash	$60,000		$60,000
Accounts Receivable	$180,000	$50,000	$230,000
Inventory	$300,000		$300,000
Fixed Assets (net)	$210,000		$210,000
Accounts Payable	($90,000)		($90,000)
Accrued Liabilities	($50,000)	($25,000)	($75,000)
Notes Payable	($420,000)		($420,000)
Equity	($350,000)		($350,000)
Revenue	($400,000)	($50,000)	($450,000)
Cost of Goods Sold	$290,000		$290,000
Salaries	$200,000	$25,000	$225,000
Payroll Taxes	$20,000		$20,000
Rent	$35,000		$35,000
Other Expenses	$15,000		$15,000
Totals	$0.00	$0.00	$0.00

Closing the Books

When closing your books at the end of a fiscal year, there are four areas that will need to be closed. These areas are temporary accounts and should be zeroed out at the end of each fiscal year.

First, create an income summary account. This is considered a holding area.

Closing the Revenue Accounts

The first area that needs to be addressed is the revenue accounts. You will either debit or credit this account to close it out and have a zero balance. Then you will either debit or credit the income summary account to add that balance to the account. Remember if you debit or credit one account you must do the opposite for the other account to keep the books balanced.

Closing the Expense Accounts

The second set of accounts are the expense accounts. You will do the same with these accounts as you did with the Revenue accounts. You must close out all expense accounts.

Balancing the Income Summary

By name, you should have an increase in the income summary for the revenue and a decrease for each of the expenses. Keep in mind that if the expenses are more than the revenue, then it will be a negative number and considered a loss. However, if the revenue is more than the expenses, then it is a gain or profit for that year.

Closing the Income Summary

The last step in closing the book is to debit or credit the income summary account and do the same to the retained earnings account, leaving a zero balance in the income summary account.

Preparing Reports

A pretty important step is to prepare the reports or financial statements. Although there are so many reports that can be created, we are going to focus on the main reports as they are what is needed for a small business.

As a bookkeeper, you will need to get very familiar with the following reports:

- Balance sheet

- Income statement

- Statement of retained earnings

- Statement of cash flow

Later in this book, we will look more closely at each one of these statements and how to read them so that you can make sense out of your businesses financial standings.

Managing the Assets, Liabilities, and Owner's Equity

Before we go too much into some of the financial reports of your business, it is important to consider three areas that you need to manage well in the area of accounting. Knowing these will make it easier to control your business finances and will ensure that you are going to be able to fill out those financial documents later on. The three main areas of accounting that you should consider include the assets, the liabilities, and the owner's equity.

Assets

The first area we are going to explore is the assets. These would be any cash that the business has on hand, as well as anything that the company could sell relatively quickly and make money on. Some of the assets that your business needs to keep track of include the following:

- Any property or real estate

- Fixed income

- Equipment

- Brokerage services

- Money market accounts

- Loans that the company made to others

- Debit or credit cards the business holds

If you run a business, you already know that you need some kind of funding to keep the doors open. Therefore, when you are looking at a financial institute to help you get that funding so you can get started, you must make sure to pick out a good bank, one which is able and is willing to give you the loan and work with you as you grow.

Working with a bank and convincing them to give you the funding that you need is important to the well-being of your business. But it can also be one of the hardest parts. You have to convince them that your business is a good one. You need to convince them that you will be able to pay them back. You need to convince them that they won't waste money by helping you out.

While each bank is going to be a little bit different, here are some of the things that most banks are going to look for:

The number of years you have been in business. The longer you have been running your business, the easier it is to get the money.

- A minimum amount of revenue. This also depends on how much money you are asking the bank for.

- A minimum FICO score. Some banks will require you to submit your personal credit before they give any funding.

- Profitability: Does the loan rely on you being able to earn a certain amount of profit to pay it back or not?

- Bankruptcy: If your business, or you personally, has filed for bankruptcy in the past, you may have to look at the rules of that bank to find out if they will still provide you with the loan.

- Credit card volume: Some loans will take a look at your credit card volume for the business before giving you a loan. This is because those kinds of loans are going to be paid off with the use of volume.

- Accounts receivable: Some types of loans, usually the alternative ones, will want to take a look at your accounts receivable when making a decision.

- Existing debt: The bank oftentimes look at the debt that your business already has and how well you have been able to manage it so far.

- Each type of loan that you go for will require different things before you can be approved. For example, a startup loan doesn't require you to be in business at all before applying while a line of credit would need at least a year in business and a small business administration loan would require that you be in business for at least two years.

You will need to make sure that you are getting all the paperwork in order before you decide to go talk to the bank. This will ensure that you are ready for them and makes it easier to get the funding that you need. A good credit score, a lower balance on any personal or business accounts, all the financial documents for the business, and information on what the funding will be used for can all be useful to the bank when making a decision.

Also, consider shopping around for a bit. You don't have to just go with one bank when it is time to go with funding. Some banks are friendlier to small businesses, and some will offer better deals to people who agree to work with them. Talking to a few different banks and finding out what they can offer to you could help you get more of the funding that you need, and could even save you money in the process.

Liabilities

The next thing we are going to look at is the different liabilities of the company. This would be anything that you still owe on, such as a loan from a bank, the amount that you owe to stockholders at the end of the quarter, or anything else that would take money away from the profits that you earn. Customer deposits and fund securities can be examples of a liability.

As a business, it is best if you are able to keep those liabilities to a minimum, although this can be hard if you are just starting out the business. No matter how good you are in the business world and no matter how well you keep the business in control, you will end up with some kind of liability. However, there are ways on how to ensure your business, as well as its assets, the protection it needs from the liabilities when they arise. Let's take a look at some of the ways that you can protect yourself against these liabilities.

Personal Liability

Even though you started your business and incorporated as a limited liability company, it doesn't mean that you won't have any personal liabilities with the business. This is rarer, but when you are starting up, there may be some things that you can do in order to get funding or to get the business off the ground that could hold you personally liable for the business. Some examples of this include the following:

- You guarantee the loan for funding for the business.

- The actions that you personally do result in the injury.

- You did something illegal with the business or committed some other crime.

- You do not operate the business in a way that makes it separate from your personal accounts.

To help protect yourself, you may want to consider having some business liability insurance. This is going to be there to protect your small business from property damage or personal injury if there is a lawsuit that should come up. There are a few different types of business liability insurance that you can choose to go with:

- Professional liability insurance: This is going to protect any business owners who provide service to their customers. It could protect you against omissions, negligence, errors, malpractice, and more. This can help protect you in case there is an accident with another person while you provide them a service so you don't end up losing all your personal assets in the process.

- Product liability insurance: This protects you against any financial loss that could occur because of defective products that cause harm to someone.

- General liability insurance: This is a general policy that will protect you against advertising claims, any claim of negligence, property damages, and injury claims.

Owner's Equity

There isn't really one set way for you to manage the owner's equity. This is going to be based off a few things including the investment you get from stocks, the money you put into the company, and the amount that you take out from the company. To handle these transactions, you will just need to use your regular bank account for business and then make sure it is linked up to your bookkeeping software.

Using Ledgers to Keep Track of Your Business Activity

L edgers and journals are going to be one of the most important parts of bookkeeping. These ledgers will hold onto the information for your bookkeeping and keeping them up to date can ensure that your accounting is done the right way. These ledgers and journals will help you to keep track of any transaction that occurs in your business so you know where they come from and so much more. Let's take a look at how each of these work and why they are so important.

Financial Journals

When it comes to journaling for your business and for bookkeeping, you are going to work with a general journal. If you aren't familiar with this general journal, you may look it over and get a bit lost on what the numbers mean and how it will impact your business. The general journal will hold a lot of information, but there are also six other journals, that can either make up this one or be used on their own depending on your business, which can help you keep track of the various transactions that you complete. These are some of the journals you can use, in addition to the general journal:

- Purchase returns journal

- Purchase journal

- Sales returns journal

- Sales journal

- Cash payments journal

- Cash receipts journal

These financial journals hold a lot of information for you. Remember that if you deal with any accounting or bookkeeping software, you will not have to deal with these journals on your own. But it is still important to know what they all are and how they can be of benefit to your business.

Cash Receipts Journal (CRJ)

When you receive any cash in your business, you will need to make sure it is recorded in the cash receipts journal. There are different categories that come with the CRJ. These categories include debtors, income, sundry, bank, ref. details, and date.

Any time that you look at your business CRJ, you will see that there are three major categories that will go on the top. The bank is going to be the total of each line and will show you the cash that was received. Income is going to be taken from any receipts that you have where you brought in money. You will also receive a receipt from your debtors any time you paid them out money. The category "sundry" is basically going to be general or miscellaneous payments that you may have.

Cash Payments Journal (CPJ)

Similar to the CRJ, the cash payments journal is going to show you where the cash has been paid out for a business. This one will also have some of the same categories as the CRJ including sundry, creditors, expenses, ref. details, bank, and date for each transaction.

If you decide that you would like to use a cash book rather than the general journal, then the CPJ is going to be a combination of your SPJ and the SRJ. This allows the cash book to show you all the payments and the receipts at the same time. When you use a petty cash fund in your business, you can keep track of this fund with the help of additional journals, and they will work on the same format as the CPJ and CRJ.

Sales Journal (SJ)

Whether your business is going to offer merchandise, services, or a combination of both, sales are going to be so important. And to help you keep track of these sales, a Sales Journal can be the tool that you want. For this kind of journal, only the income on credit will show up.

Once this is paid, and the business receives payment or cash for the service, then it will be recorded in the cash receipts journal. Some of the main categories that are present in the sales journal include services rendered, ref., debtor, and date.

Sales Return Journal (SRJ)

Every time your company sells a product or merchandise, you will occasionally deal with a customer returning the item. When one of these returns happens, you will need to record this return in the sales returns journal about where it had been originally sold to. The categories that you will find in the SRL includes the sales returns, ref., debtor, and date.

Purchases Journal (PJ)

When the business has some type of inventory, you will also work with the purchases journal. This is the journal that you will use when your business purchases inventory on credit. The PJ is only going to apply to the inventory you have. This means you will not purchase all your assets here. Only the inventory that you purchase using credit should be put on the purchases journal. The categories that come with this journal includes purchases, ref., creditor, and the date.

Purchase Returns Journal (PRJ)

Just like when you use the SRJ, the purchase returns journal is going to record any of the merchandise that the business purchased on credit and is then needed to be able to return to the merchandiser. The categories that you will put on your PRJ include purchases returns, ref., creditor, and date.

General Journal (GJ)

The general journal is the tool that will hold onto all the transactions that your business makes. It will hold onto the information that is found in the other six journals that we talked about. This is a great way to put all the information about transactions in your business in one place.

The Ledgers

When you work with double-entry accounting and bookkeeping, there are three main categories of ledgers that you should look at. These will include the following:

- General ledger

- Accounts receivable ledger

- Accounts payable ledger

It may seem like you are taking up a lot of time to record all your entries in these ledgers twice. But you want to organize these transactions in both the journals we talked about before as well as in the ledger accounts to help you keep track of things.

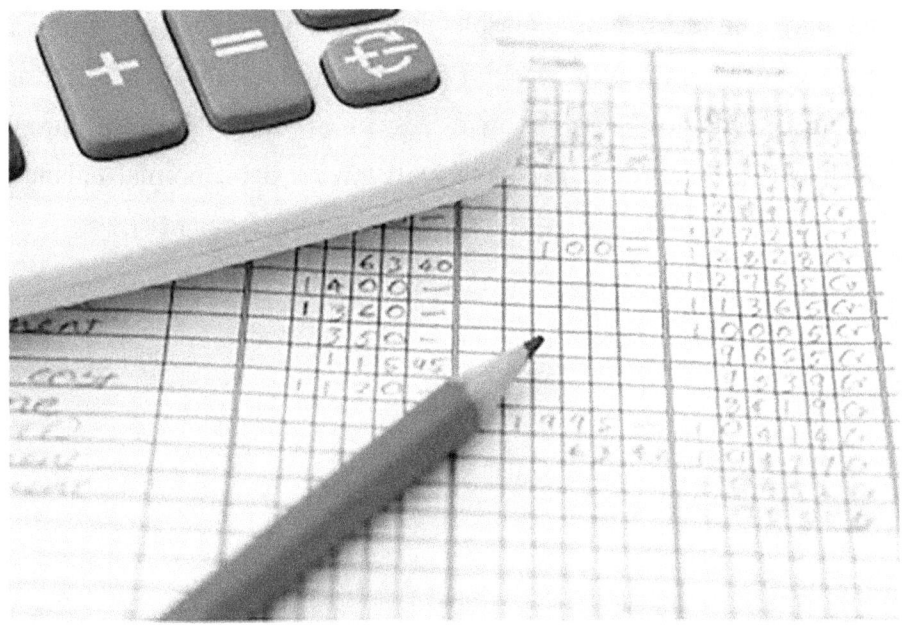

The General Ledger

As soon as you set up the bookkeeping for your business, a chart of accounts is created. Each account on this chart will have a reference number assigned to it. This helps you to keep track of the different transactions that happen, regardless of whether they are found in the journal or on the ledger. This general ledger is important to help you keep track of your transactions in one place, and when you combine it together with the journals from above, you will be able to keep track of everything financial about your business.

Accounts Receivable Ledger and the Accounts Payable Ledger

These two ledgers are considered subsidiary ledger accounts. These are the accounts that are, in addition to your general ledger, will mainly be used so you can accurately track the receivables and the payables of your business.

You may end up having multiple accounts that belong to vendors whom you owe money to or who owe money to you. Each of these accounts needs to have its own ledgers in order to keep things organized. The accounts receivable will have a debit normal balance while the accounts payable will have a credit normal balance.

Dealing with Depreciation in Your Business

At some point when you start on your business, you will need to purchase equipment to help you get the work done. You will need this equipment to last for a few years. However, over the years of its usage, it is going to end up losing its value.

Let's look at an example of this. You purchase a computer for your business that has Windows 7 on it and all the other programs that you need to get things done. This computer costs you $575. After owning and maintaining this computer, it starts to break, and you need to find parts.

Over that time, your depreciation went down from $575 to closer to $50. And since technology is moving so fast as it advances, you find that you can no longer get the parts that you need. Now your depreciation of $50 is considered a recycling fee.

From this example, you can see that the equipment is going to lose its value, and we need to calculate this into your bookkeeping somehow. The depreciation can sometimes be an annual income tax deduction. It will be something that you will list as an expense on the income statement. This is a good deduction that is an advantage to you, and you can get this by filing the Form 4562 when you file your tax return.

There are a few guidelines that the property needs to meet ahead of time to claim this depreciation deduction. Some of these requirements include the following:

- You must actually own the property. It is impossible to depreciate capital improvements for a property that you lease.

- The property must be something that you use for business or to produce income. If you use it for personal and business use, then you are not allowed to deduce the property based only on the business use of the property.

- The property that you are trying to deduct needs to have a reasonable lifespan that is longer than a year.

Even if the property you want to deduct ends up meeting all these requirements, it may not qualify for the deduction. Here are some of the properties that you are not able to deduct:

- Any property that is placed into service and then disposed of the same year.

- Any equipment that you use to build capital improvements. You are able to add in allowable depreciation on the equipment during the construction based on improvements.

- Certain term interests.

For the most part, most of the property that you get and use for business purposes can be depreciated. You are able to depreciate a lot of your property, including equipment, furniture, vehicles, machinery, and buildings. You can't depreciate land, though, because it is expected that you will use that land for the whole lifetime of your business, and it never depreciates in value to you. The building that is on the land can be depreciated when it is time to do taxes that year.

You must take the time to identify which items you want to depreciate and deduct when you are filing your taxes. You will be able to do this with the Form 4562 to help you get started. This ensures that you are properly depreciating any of the property that you use. Some of the items that are found on this Form 4562 include these:

- Depreciable basis of the property

- Whether there are any bonuses that you qualify for in the first year of depreciation

- Whether you elect to expense out any portion of the asset

- Whether the property is listed property

- Class life of the asset

- Depreciation method for your property

The next question is all about how you are supposed to calculate what the depreciation of the property is. There are two main methods that you can use to do this. These include tax depreciation and book depreciation.

Book Depreciation

To start with, you can work with book depreciation. This is used often for bookkeeping and accounting purposes. The goal of using this depreciation type is to match the cost of an asset with the revenue that it earns over the period of its lifetime. The common method that you will use for this method is known as the straight-line method. This is calculated with one of the two formulas that are below:

- Annual depreciation = (Cost – Residual Value) / Useful Life

- Annual depreciation = (Cost – Residual Value) * Rate of depreciation.

There are several categories that you will need to fill in for both of these in order to get the answers that you need. The different parts defined are below:

- Cost: This is the original amount that you paid for the equipment or the property.

- Residual value: This is sometimes called the scrap value. This is the question of what will be the value of the property or equipment at the end of its use.

- Useful life: This is the amount of time that you plan to use and keep the equipment before you get rid of it or upgrade to something else.

- The rate of depreciation: This is the percentage of the useful life span that is used in an accounting period.

Tax Depreciation
There are a lot of different methods that you can use to calculate the depreciation of the property. This means that you are not stuck working with just one type if you don't like it or if it doesn't work for your bookkeeping needs. When you are working on your taxes,

though, the IRS likes to work with the accelerated depreciation method the best.

This is a method that will return more of your money in the first year or two of the asset's life, rather than expanding it out through the years. There are a few different methods that can be used to help with accelerated depreciation.

The first method is the declining balance depreciation. This is going to use the following formula to come up with the amount of depreciation for your property:

- Declining balance depreciation = Rate * Net book value

You can also choose to work with what is known as the double declining balance method to help you come up with the depreciation. The formula to use for this one is:

- Double declining rate = 2/useful life

- Double declining balance depreciation = net book value * 2/useful life

When you are working on the depreciation of an item or property, make sure that you keep all the receipts. There may be a time when you need to prove how much the worth of the item is, where you bought it, and so on. Having this information present and written out in a receipt will make it easier for the auditors (if any show up), your accountant, or your bookkeeper to check to make sure that you are getting the right amount of depreciation and that there are no mistakes at tax time.

The depreciation of your property can help you save money at tax time. You can regain some of the value of that item back throughout the years in your taxes, as long as the property ends up depreciating and you use it for your business use. If you are uncertain about whether or not you are able to depreciate an item from your business or how much you are able to get from depreciation, make sure to talk to your accountant to help you here.

How to Adjust Any Entry

As you are working with your small business, you may find that there are times when you need to adjust some of the entries that you put in for bookkeeping. These journal entries will be able to turn your accounting records into accrual-based accounting. These are the entries that you will want to make prior to issuing the financial statements.

In many cases, when you want to adjust an entry, you are doing it because you need to fix some of your expenses. However, you may need to use this for other things as well, including making adjustments for revenue. Basically, there are two scenarios where adjusting entry is needed before the financial statements are issued, and these include the following:

1. When nothing has been put into the accounting records for a certain revenue or expenses. These revenues or expenses did occur, and they should be included in the current balance sheet or income statement for that period, so an adjustment is necessary.

2. When there has been an entry into the records, but the amount needs to be divided up because it occurs through more than one accounting period.

Asset Accounts

Any time that you are trying to make some adjustments to the entries that you have, you need to take the time to assure that both the income statement and the balance sheet are done properly so that they check out with each other. While we will talk about both of these financial statements in a later chapter, this basically means that both these statements need to be up to date based on the accrual basis of accounting.

The best way to go through and do this is to examine and then review each of the balances that are on your balance sheet. Let's take a look at the following example and then break it down to get a better idea of what is going on. Remember, this is based on the account balances that were done before any of the adjustments were added. The different areas that we will focus on here will include the following:

- Cash: $1,800

- Accounts Receivable: $4,600

- Allowance for doubtful accounts: $0

- Supplies: $1,100

- Prepared insurance: $1,500

- Accumulated depreciation equipment: $7,500

- Equipment: $25,000

Let's break this down now that we have all the numbers. Looking at the general ledger, we'll see that the cash account is showing there is a balance of $1,800 in cash. However, before you use this information to create your balance sheet, there are two questions that you need to ask yourself. First, ask whether the $1,800 is the true amount of cash or not? Second, ask if this agrees with what was figured based on your bank reconciliation.

If the cash doesn't match with what you found out when you did the bank reconciliation, then you need to go through and make some adjustments so that the balance sheet has the right information. Some examples of needing to do this would be to check printing charges, banking fees, or service charges. These entries need to be added to the cash account so that it matches up with your bank statements.

Then you need to take a look at the accounts receivable. For this account, you need to take a look at any of the unpaid invoices that you have. These can be found on the subsidiary ledger for accounts receivable. For this, we are going to assume that the $4,600 that we had above is accurate for all the amounts that were not paid as of yet.

The balance sheets will need to report all the amounts. This should also include the money that has not yet been paid but is still due to the business. This can also go for all the revenue that has been billed at that time as well. After a review, you find out that $3,000 of services has been earned. This was dated as something that occurred on December 31, but it was not billed until January 20. In order to have that information show up on your December financial statements, you would need to go through and make an adjusting entry.

Remember that when you do your entries, they all need to have at least one credit and one debit. The two accounts that you would do in this will be the service revenue and the accounts receivable. The accounts receivable will have the normal debit balance, and it will be part of your balance sheet accounts. The service revenues have a normal credit balance and also part of the income statement accounts.

When we take a look at the previous balance that we had of $4,600 for this area and then we make the adjusting entry for the $3,000 that needs to be added in, then the new balance on this account is going to be $7,600.

Now we need to work on the allowances for doubtful accounts. If you take a look at your information here, you will notice that this account is not one that is listed on your balance sheet. The reason for this is because it has a balance of $0. It is common for an account that has a balance of $0 to not show up on the balance sheet because it is just going to pretty much take up space.

At one point, there is a possibility that your business has some accounts that have not been collected. The reasons for this can vary. Instead of reducing the accounts receivable by issuing a credit on the ledgers, you would add it to this category.

To take a look at this, let's say that your business has $600 that is not going to be collected. This means that you would want to report that $600 in the allowance for doubtful account. There are going to be two accounts that need to be brought in for this transaction. You will have this allowance for doubtful accounts on the balance sheet, and this account will have a credit normal balance. Then the other account is going to be the bad debts expense that is on the income statement. This account is going to have a normal debit balance.

As you go through your balance sheet, you need to remember which accounts are going to be affected and which ones will have either a normal debit or credit. From here, you should take some time and practice doing your own bookkeeping. Try to figure out the rest of the adjusting entries for the asset accounts. These are the numbers that you should use for getting this done and getting some practice:

- Supplies are $1,100.

- Adjusting entry is $275. The balance for supplies will be $725 and the accounts that you will use to get this done will be supplies and supplies expense.

- Prepaid insurance is $1,500.

- The adjusting entry is going to be $900. The balance for this prepaid insurance will be $600, and the accounts that you will use are insurance expense and prepaid insurance.

- Equipment is $25,000.

- You do not need to do any adjusting entries here.

- Accumulated depreciation equipment is $7,500.

- Adjusting entry is going to be $15,000. The balance for the accumulated depreciation equipment is going to be $9,000, and the accounts that you will use for this one will be the accumulated depreciation equipment and the depreciation expense equipment.

Adjusting the Entries with Liability Accounts

As you take a review of the accounts that are on your balance sheet, it is not enough to just take a look at the assets and then stop there. The liability accounts should also be reviewed. You want to go through and check out these accounts using the same methods that you used with the assets. The steps to doing this would include the following:

- Notes payable: $5,000

- There is no adjusting entry that is needed here.

- Interest payable: $0

- Adjusting entry is $25. The balance for the interest payable is going to be $25, and the accounts that are involved with this are the interest expense and the interest payable.

- Accounts payable: $2,500

- Adjusting entry is $1,000. The balance for the accounts payable will be $3,500 and the accounts involved are accounts payable and repairs and maintenance expense.

- Wages payable is $1,200.

- Adjusting entry is $300. The balance of wages payable is going to be $1,500, and the accounts that you will use with this one are the wages payable and the wages expense.

- Unearned revenues will be $1,300.

- Adjusting entry is $800. The balance for your unearned revenues will be $500, and the accounts involved will include unearned revenues and service revenues.

When you do this, remember that the normal balance for each of the account is going to be affected. As you go through and adjust the entries, and when you do not know the normal balance for both transactions, you should try to find the one that you do know. There is going to be a credit and debit for each transaction made always. If it has a credit normal balance and then the adjustment ends up increasing the account, then you need to also go through and debit the other account.

The Different
Financial Statements

As we have mentioned a few times in this guidebook, there are some financial documents that are important to your business. These documents are going to help you keep your finances in line, help you know whether you are making accurate entries into the ledger, and can even assist you when you need to bring in investors or lenders to grow your business.

As an owner of a small business, you need to have a good understanding of some of these basic statements so you can really get a good look at where the business stands financially. This is where it is extremely important for you to always communicate with the bookkeeping.

There are actually quite a few different financial statements that you could look at. The one that you want to work with will depend on what you are interested in finding out. But the most common ones and the ones that are often seen as the most important include these:

- The cash flow statement

- The owner's equity statement

- The income statement

- The balance sheet

These are considered the big four because they are going to give you a good picture of where your business is standing financially. They are also the statements that you need to show your investors to make decisions about whether they will work with you or not. Let's take a look at each one and see how they work and why they are so important for your business.

You must make sure that you fill out these financial statements on a regular basis. Most companies will do one each quarter of their business, and then they do this at the end of the year. There are several benefits to doing this. First, it is required for all publicly traded companies through the SEC. You need to submit these four documents to the SEC at these times to remain on the stock exchange.

You will find that a lot of your investors and lenders will take a look at these financial statements. They are able to get a good view of your financial state and can make smart decisions about whether they want to invest in you or give you a loan. Without this information, the investors and the lenders won't even consider you. So even if the SEC didn't require that you submit this information to them, it could still be useful if you need a business loan to fund something, like new equipment or expansion or to help convince investors that your business is a good option.

Another benefit of using these financial statements is that they give you a good view of your financial statement in the business. You will be able to fill them out pretty easily if you have been keeping good records through the other tips that we talked about. You can then compare this information with the financial statements that you completed in previous quarters and years to let you know the trends of your financial state and make good decisions to prepare you for the future.

The Balance Sheet

The first financial document we will look at is the balance sheet. This one is going to use the formula assets = liabilities + equity. Within this particular statement, you will see that these three areas are divided up to show which of your business accounts are listed under the owner's equity, liabilities, and assets.

The owner's equity will represent the earnings that are retained for your business. You will see that all the accounts that are on this balance sheet do not have to keep a $0 balance. Generally, the accounts with $0 balance are ones that are not on the balance sheet.

You can pick from two types of formats for your balance sheet. You can pick from either the horizontal or the vertical formats. Most businesses prefer to work with the vertical format. But if you want to work more with the accounting equation from before, you will want to work with the horizontal format.

Based on the assets that your business has, the business is going to be balanced in all the obligations of a business financially. This will include investments and any retained earnings. Think about it this way. Assets are the means a business uses to operate. Owner's equity and liabilities are the two main ways that you can support these assets.

The balance sheet is going to be the financial statement that will report all the assets and liabilities of the company as well as the shareholders' equity, basing this from a specific point in time. It is a going to provide you with a basis for computing rates of return and then evaluating the capital structure of the business.

The neat thing about the balance sheet is that it is really good for providing a snapshot of the company, what that company owes and owns, and also some information about the amount that has been invested by shareholders. It can go in depth or just give an overview of the finances of the business.

Many investors and lenders will take a look at the balance sheet. They do need to look at some of the other financial statements to get the best view of how the company is doing financially. But the balance sheet is a good place for the lenders and the investors to look to in order to see a summary or a snapshot of the company before going further.

Interpreting the balance sheet is not meant to be difficult. This statement is a snapshot that represents the state of the company financially in just one moment of time. By itself, it is not going to show you the trends of the company that have played out over time. Because of this, when you are attempting to interpret the balance sheet, you need to compare it with some previous balance sheets. So if you are looking at the balance sheet for the fourth quarter of the company, you should compare to the balance sheets for the third, second, and first quarters as well so you can see the numbers and the trends over the past year.

In addition, it is a good idea to take those balance sheets and then compare them to other businesses that are considered to work in the same industry. This gives you a good idea of whether the company is doing well compared to the trends in the industry or not. Don't compare the balance sheet of a company to those in different industries because each industry will have its own approaches to financing and this can get confusing.

Now that you know a bit more about the balance sheet, it is important to know what accounts need to be listed in each section. These are the owner's equity, liability, and assets. Let's divide each part up to see what will be inside each one on the balance sheet.

Current Assets

The items that you put inside the current assets are the ones that will have a lifespan of a year or less. The business then plans to convert those assets into cash. Some of the items that you can put into the current assets part of the balance statement include these:

- Short-term obligations that you owe to the clients

- Accounts receivable

- US Treasuries

- Cash

- Cash and cash equivalents

- Raw materials

- Inventory

Noncurrent Assets

These assets are the ones that can't be turned into cash as easily. These are the ones that are expected to be turned into cash within a year, or they could have a longer life span of more than a year. These are the ones that will usually have depreciation associated with them as well. Some examples of these types of assets include the following:

- Copyright

- Patents

- Goodwill

- Intangible assets

- Land

- Buildings

- Computers

- Machinery

- Tangible assets

Liabilities

When you are looking at your liabilities, you are going to consider this as the obligations that the business owes to others. Just like assets, these can include both long-term and current liabilities. These are some of the liabilities that will be found in this column of the balance statement:

- Nondebts that are more than one year old

- Debts that are more than one year

- Long-term liabilities

- Accounts payable

- Paid within a year

- Current liabilities

Owner's Equity

This is the money that the owner has invested inside of their business. The retained earnings that are shown on your income statement will be transferred into the owner's equity at the end of your fiscal year. The owner's equity is going to show the net worth of the business. You will have a capital account or a drawing account. The capital account is going to be any money invested or earned by the business. The drawing account is going to be the money that is withdrawn from the business.

The Income Statement

When you first take a look at the business statement, there is a lot of information, and it can seem scary. However, once you know what is inside of it, you will find that this statement can be really useful. The income statement is going to take a closer look at all the sales and all the expenses of that business. The business can usually choose to do this quarterly and annually through their fiscal year to keep track of things.

An income statement is another financial statement that is going to be responsible for reporting a company's financial performance over a specific period of accounting. The financial performance of a company will be assessed by providing a summary to lenders and investors about how the business will incur all its revenues and expenses through both its nonoperating and operating activities.

The income statement is often going to be known as the profit and loss statement, and it is one of the three financial statements that need to be present in the annual report of the company as well as the 10-K. All public companies will need to submit these documents legally to the SEC and the investor public. The other two sheets that are submitted at the same time will be the cash flows statement and the balance sheet.

These three are important because they can provide the investors and the lenders with a lot of information about the state of finances of a business, but the income statement is unique because it is the only one that will summarize the sales and the net income of the company.

Unlike what you would do with the company balance sheet, the income statement is going to provide the performance information about a certain time. While the balance sheet will just say how the business is at the exact time the business owner filled out the sheet, the income statement is going to provide information over a year, a quarter, or a year based on the way that the company records this information. The income statement is going to start off with the sales of the company and then will work its way down to the net income and then the earnings per share.

There are two main parts that need to be present on the income statement, no matter what type of company you are running. These two parts are the nonoperating and the operating.

With the operating portion of this financial statement, you will disclose all the information about any revenues and expenses that the company incurred directly from regular business operations. For example, if you are a business that sells sports equipment, you would make your money by selling these pieces of equipment. This information would be recorded in the operating section of this statement.

The income statement also needs to include the nonoperating section. This is going to disclose all the information about expenses and revenue for any activities that aren't a part of the regular operations of the company. If your company sells investment securities or real estate in addition to your regular work, then you would list any profits you made from those sales in the nonoperating section.

You may hear many different terms when it comes to the income statement. You may hear about income, earnings, and profits. These all mean the same thing so keep this in mind when you hear them. There are also two basic formats that you can use with the income statement, the single-step format or the multistep format.

The Multistep Format

These are some of the parts that are going to be shown in the multistep format:

- Net sales

- Cost of sales

- Gross income

- Selling, general, and administrative expenses

- Taxes

- Pretax income

- Other income and expenses

- Operating income

- Net income after taxes

The Single-Step Format

Some of the steps that come with the single-step format include the following:

- Net income

- Taxes

- Pretax income

- Other income and expenses

- Research and development expenses

- Marketing and administrative

- Materials and production

- Net sales

You can choose the method that works best for your business and will include all the information about your own finances.

Statement of Owner's Equity

The next financial statement to look at is the owner's equity statement. This is a financial document that can be used on its own as a separate statement, or it can be something included in the income statements or the balance sheet. It is sometimes also known as a Statement of Retained Earnings. This is the statement that will let you show the standing of your business earnings.

Often you are going to see this type of statement in a corporation that has a lot of shareholders and pays out dividends. But you can still find it useful with your small business in order to show your financial standings and your retained earnings. The main reason to use this statement is to release all this financial information to the public, giving the public the information they need to decide if they would like to invest in the business. It is also a good tool to analyze how healthy your business is.

The statement of owner's equity will represent the value of a business after it has met all its obligations through a specific period of time. This statement is responsible for showing the movement of capital throughout that company and will reflect the amount that the owner or owners invested into the company along with any profits that the business has been able to generate that is then reinvested directly into the company. The reinvested income will be known as retained earnings on this sheet.

This statement is going to report the changes in the owner's equity over a certain period, and this period is usually going to be for each year. As a small business, there is a chance that you won't need to use this statement because smaller businesses are more likely to report the retained earnings on the balance sheet instead.

If you do decide that your business needs to prepare the statement of owner's equity, you will want to prepare it after you are done with the income statement. This is because this particular statement will need to have the net income or the net loss for the period. But you can prepare this before the balance sheet because the owner's equity will need to be on the balance sheet as well.

This statement is a good one to use because it will help you to see the financial health of a business. It can also give you some insight into whether or not the business has sufficient cash flow to help fund its own operations without needing the aid of any outside investment.

Most of the time, you don't want to see a company reinvest their profits into the business because this can show that they are not doing a great job of handling their cash flow. But if the business is growing really quickly, the owners may decide to invest some capital to help fund additional wages, accounts receivable, and inventory to help them keep up. This is acceptable because that money will easily be made back shortly once they catch up a bit.

The problem is if the business is not able to support itself financially without these capital infusions. If the business does this statement and it is not able to support itself without these infusions of capital, then the creditors are not likely to work with the business, and it can be hard to get the loan that you need to run your business.

Cash Flow Statement

The cash flow statement is going to show you the flow of cash that comes into and out of your business. It is able to do this by splitting this information up into four parts. These parts include the following:

Operating activities: This will convert the items that are found on your prepared income statement from the accrual basis of accounting to cash.

- Investing activities: This lists the purchases and the sales that occur from any of your long-term investments, your property, or your plant and equipment.

- Financing activities: This is the report that will show the issuance and the repurchase of company bonds and stocks. It will also include information about payments of the dividends.

- Supplemental information: This is the report will show any exchange of significant items. These are items that do not involve any cash and can report the number of income interests and taxes that the company pays out.

The statement of cash flows, also known as the cash flow statement, is a financial statement that most businesses need to use in order to summarize the amount of cash, as well as cash equivalents, that enter and leave the company.

This statement is important for measuring how well a company is able to manage the position it has with cash. What this means is how well the company is able to generate cash or profits in order to fund any operating expenses it has and any debt obligations it needs to pay out. The cash flow statement works along with the income statement and the balance sheet, and it has been a mandatory part of financial reports for a company since 1987.

The cash flow statement is going to be very useful for a company. It is going to allow lenders and investors to have a better understanding of how a company's operations are going, where the money for a company comes from, and how that money is being spent. It is so important because it will ensure that lenders and investors have the right information to determine whether a particular company is financially secure or not.

Creditors will often use this information to help them determine the amount of cash that the company has readily available. The company needs to have this money to help them pay off debts and pay their operating expenses. If the company doesn't have enough cash based on their debts and operating costs, it may not look that great for the company, and the creditor may not offer the loan to them.

The main components that come with the cash flow statement of the company include these:

- Cash from all the operating activities.

- Cash from investing activities of the company.

- Cash from any financing activities that the business has.

- Any noncash activities—these are sometimes included but will depend on the business.

It is important to know that the cash flow statement is going to hold different information, compared to the balance sheet and the income statement. This is because it is not going to include the amount of the future cash that comes in and goes out. This information will be recorded on credit. What this means is that the cash of the company is not the same thing as the net income, which is found on the balance sheet and income statement, which includes sales and the cash sales made on credit.

These sections can hold onto a lot of different information, and the parts that you fill in will depend on what your business does. Let's break down each of these sections to help see what information needs to go inside each one when you do your bookkeeping.

Operating Activities

- Other liabilities that are current

- Unearned revenues

- Income taxes payable

- Interest payable

- Payroll taxes payable

- Wages payable

- Accounts payable

- Notes payable

- Other current assets

- Prepaid insurance

- Supplies

- Inventory

- Accounts receivable

Investing Activities

- Vehicles

- Furniture and fixtures

- Equipment

- Buildings

- Land

- Any long-term investments

Financing Activities

- Treasury stock

- Retained earnings

- Paid-in capital from your treasury stock

- Paid-in capital in excess of par-preferred stock

- Preferred stock

- Deferred income taxes

- Bonds payable

- Notes payable (ones that are usually due after a year)

Supplemental Information

This is going to include anything else that shows the flow of cash into and out of the business that is not covered in the above categories.

The Income Statement

As we mentioned a little bit before, accounting is going to be in charge of creating a few important financial reports. They are able to use the information they are provided by the bookkeeper and then will put that information into these statements so it is easier to understand and read through.

These financial statements are very important to a business. First off, they are required by the SEC for any company that is publicly traded so having an accountant go through your records and create them can be important. These documents are often seen by potential investors and lenders. Having these documents available can ensure that the investors will choose to purchase your stocks, or that the lenders are willing to loan you money if it is needed at some point.

First, we will get started with the income statement. This is the statement that is going to be part of the financial statement that is required to report a company's financial performance over a certain amount of time. Sometimes, this is each month or some other time frame, but most of the time, it will be over a quarter and then done when the business reaches its fiscal year.

The financial performance of a company is going to be analyzed by providing a good summary of how the business will incur both its expenses and its revenues. This information comes from both the nonoperating and operating activities. This document is also important because it will show the net profit or the net loss that the business incurred over a specific accounting period.

How to Break Down the Income Statement

This document can go by other names, including the statement of revenue and expense, or as the profit and loss statement. It is also one of the major financial statements that a business is going to present in its 10-K and its annual report. All the public companies need to submit these legal documents to the SEC or the Securities and Exchange Commission. These also need to be released out to the investor public.

Along with the other two documents, we will discuss here, the income statement will provide any lenders and investors with all the information they need about how the company is doing financially. However, the income statement is unique because it will be the only one out of the three that can also provide a summary of the net income and the company sales at that specific time.

Income Statement

While the income statement is presented along with using the balance sheet, it will be able to cover time a little bit differently. The first sheet will just cover one moment out of time. The moment that the accountant is preparing the balance sheet is the moment that will show up on that statement. However, the income statement is a bit different because it will show you information over a period of time and not just how it is doing at one specific time. This period is usually over a month, a quarter, or even up to a year. It will begin with the sales of the business and then keeps working down until it reaches the net earnings and the net income of each share for that company.

76

When you work on the income statement, there are two parts that need to be present; the nonoperating and the operating. First, we need to look at the operating costs that are found on the income statement. These operating costs are going to list out and disclose the information that concerns the expenses and the revenues that come right from regular business operations. If you run a fast food restaurant, the operating costs could include the amount that you made selling the food and drink items at the establishment. You can list out all the income and the earnings that you made that directly relate to your business in this part.

You also need to include any nonoperating income on the income statement. This section is going to show the revenue and the expenses that the business does, but which don't directly come with the regular operations of the business. So if the fast food restaurant rents out parking spots for the apartments next door to use, and they make money from that, then this information would go in the nonoperating section of your income statement.

Uses for the Income Statement

There are many different uses for the income statement. First, many analysts will use this statement in order to get the data they need to calculate financial ratios. They can use this to get earnings before interest taxes and amortization, earnings before you pay taxes and interest, any operating profit, the gross profit, the return on an asset, and the return on equity. As you can see, there are a lot of different numbers that can come on the income statement, and analysts will use these to figure out the financial health of the company.

Companies can also use the income statement. It is common for them to present the income statement in a common-sized format, where each line item will be shown as a percent of the sales. When it is done in this format, it makes things easier on an analyst to see which of the expenses of a company make up the biggest portion of the sales. In addition, analysts can use this income statement to help compare how the company is doing from one year to another or from one quarter to another. One thing you will notice about the income statement is that it will typically have two or three years of data about the company, so it is easier for comparisons when needed.

Many investors will choose to work with the income statement to help them determine whether one company or another is the right one for them to invest in. They can take a look at how much money the business makes, how much debt the company has, and whether these numbers are reasonable or if they show signs that the business is having trouble. Presenting a good income statement can make a difference in how many investors you attract into the company and how valuable your stocks are.

Your lenders, or potential lenders, will also take a look at the income statement. Even if you are making good profits, there may be times when you need to get a loan. You may need to do an expansion, hire some extra employees for a busy season, or do something else that will require a loan. Having a good income statement can make it easier to get the loan that you need when you need it the most.

The Methods for Creating Your Income Statement

There are two main formats that you can choose for your income statement to help present your financial information. These include the single-step and the multistep format. In the multistep format, there will be four different measures that can look at profitability, and these will be shown at the right junctions for the operations of the company. These junctions will include after tax, pretax, operating, and gross.

When you work with the single-step option, your gross income, as well as the operating income, will not be shown. You can choose to use the information that is shown to calculate these numbers. This method will have you take the sales and then minus the materials and production to be what equals the gross income of the company. You can then subtract the marketing and administrative, and also the R&D expenses if you have them, from your gross income to come up with the operating income for the business.

This is pretty easy to figure out, so it's not a big deal to use this one if you wish. If you are an investor looking through the income statement, you need to realize that this statement is going to look at any revenues for the business at the time they are realized. This means they look at when the goods are on their way to the customer, whenever a service is rendered, or when the business incurs the expenses.

Let's take a look at some of the categories that will be found in each of these methods to help you see how they are similar and how they are different from each other:

Multistep Format	Single-Step Format
Net sales	Net sales
Cost of sales	Materials and production

Gross income	Marketing and administrative
Selling, general and administrative expenses (SG&A)	Research and development expenses
Operating income	Other income and expenses
Other income and expenses	Pretax income
Pretax income	Taxes
Taxes	Net income
Net income (after tax)	

You can use one of these two methods to help you create your own income statement as long as you stick with one and don't get the parts mixed up. You may also need to change a few things around on some of the other financial documents to get the answers that you want, but both of these will work for a business. If you are unsure about which method to go with, you may want to talk to a professional accountant and see what they recommend for your business or your industry.

The Accounts Found on the Income Statement

Most accountants are going to work on the multiformat method when it comes to writing out the income statement. This can make it easier for the numbers to show up and can ensure that investors are going to be able to see the information right out front rather than having to go through and figure out the numbers on their own. Some of the parts that come with the multistep format on the income statement include these:

- Net sales: This can also be known as sales or revenue. This is the term that refers to the value of the sales of a company or its services to the customer. Even though the bottom line of the company or the net income often ends up getting more investors to look at it, the very top is where you will see the income part start. Also, profit margins on the existing products of that company will eventually reach a maximum that will be hard for the company to improve on. This basically means that the company will not be able to grow faster than any revenue from the business.

- Cost of sales: This is how much it costs the business for any goods or products sold. For a manufacturing company, the cost of sales will be an expense that had to be taken on to deal with everything that helps the product be produced. The depreciation expense is going to be in this part as well. With retailers and wholesalers, you will see that this is the purchase of merchandise that is sold in the store. In a business that is service businesses, the cost would be how much it cost the business to offer their services to the customer.

- Gross profit: This can also be known as gross margin or gross income. The gross profit of a company is going to not only show the difference that shows up between your net sales and what the sales cost the company. The gross profits can provide you with all the resources to cover all the expenses for the company. The greater and the more stable this gross margin is, the greater potential there is for a good bottom line for the company.

- Selling, general, and administrative expenses: This one is going to be referred to as the SG&A in the accounting world. This account is going to hold onto all the operating expenses for the company.

- Operating income: When you deduct SG&A from the gross profit of the company, you will get the operating income. This is an important figure because it can show the earnings from the company's normal operations before the nonoperating income and the costs like special items, taxes, and interest expenses. Income at this level, which is often seen as a more reliable number, is going to be used more often by financial analysts instead of using the net income to help measure how profitable a business is.

- Interest expense: This is the item that will show the cost of the company borrowing money. Sometimes, a company can choose to record their net figure here to hold onto interest expense and the interest income when they have invested funds.

- Pretax income: Another indicator that can show how well a business is doing is to look at the earnings that are garnered before the income tax expense. Numerous techniques are there to help a company to minimize or avoid the taxes that they report on their income. Since these are actions that don't help the operations of that particular business, the analysts may want to choose to go with pretax income because it can be more accurate at measuring the profitability of that company.

- Income taxes: The income tax is often not going to be the amount that the company actually pays. Since there are deductions and other things for the company to do to reduce their taxes, this number is just an estimate. It often goes into an account that is created to help the company cover their taxes, but they can often get it lower.

- Special items: There are some events that can occasionally be charged against the income of the company. The company can identify these as discontinued operations, unusual items, or restructuring charges. These are write-offs that should just be one-time events. Any investor that looks at your company should look at these items and consider them when looking at a company because sometimes, they can distort the evaluation.

- Net income: This is also known as the net earnings or the net profit. This is going to be the bottom line for the company, and it is going to be the most common indicator of how profitable the company is. If the expenses exceed the income, then you will have a net loss. After that, the company pays out the dividends that are preferred stockholders if there are any, and then the net income is going to add to the equity position of the company and turns into retained earnings. There is sometimes some supplemental data presented for net income on the basis of potential conversion of stocks, basis of shares outstanding, and warrants.

Comprehensive income: This concept is going to consider the effects of some things including unrealized gains and losses, the minimum pension liability, foreign currency adjustments, and more. The investment community is mostly going to keep focusing on the net income figure that we talked about before. The adjustment items that come with comprehensive income will all relate to a market that is volatile or an economic event that is out of control of the management at the time. The impact at that specific time can be huge, but over time, they are going to even out and won't matter that much.

The Balance Sheet

A balance sheet is going to show the assets of the company, the liabilities of the company, and the net worth, or the owner's equity. The balance sheet will work along with the other financial documents that we have talked about in order to show a complete picture of the financial state of that company. If you hold onto stocks of that company, it is a good idea to understand more about the balance sheet, such as how it is structured, the best ways to look over and understand the sheet, and even tips for reading through the balance sheet.

How Can I Use this Financial Document?

The balance sheet is going to be split up into two parts. These two parts are going to be based on an equation, and they must either end up equaling each other or coming out so that they are balanced, or something is wrong with your numbers. The formula that is needed to work with the balance sheet will include this:

Assets = Liabilities + Shareholder's Equity

What all this means is that all the assets, or the money used to operate the company, need to be balanced out by the financial obligations of the company, along with any of the equity investment that comes back to that company, and then they will be known as that company's retained earnings.

The assets are important because they are what the company will use in order to operate the business. The equity and the liabilities are going to be what will support those assets. The owner's equity, which can be known as the shareholder's equity, if the company is publicly traded, will include any of the money that the shareholders invested in that company. It can also include any retained earnings as well. This is important because it is going to represent the funding sources for that particular business.

One way that the balance sheet is different than the income statement we talked about before is that the balance sheet we talked about earlier is more of a snapshot that showcases the financial position of that company right then and there. If the accountant does this financial document on May 21, 2018, then the balance sheet will show where the company is on that date. It won't cover February 21 to May 21. It just shows May 21.

The Balance Sheet for the Securities and Exchange Commission

Just like the bank wants you to put together a balance sheet to take a look at whether they think you can do well with any credit they offer, the government is going to require that any company that is traded publicly will put together a balance sheet, usually each quarter, to show to their shareholders.

This balance sheet can be important because it will allow all potential and current investors to see a good snapshot of the finances of that company. In addition to some other things, the balance sheet is going to show you all the value of the stuff that the company owns, right down to the office supplies that the employees use, the amount of debt that the company is taking care of right now, and how much inventory is in the warehouse. It can even tell the investors about how much money the business will have available to work with through the short-term.

This balance statement is going to be one of the first financial statements that you should analyze when you want to see the value of the company. Before you can learn how to analyze this balance sheet, it is important to know how it is structured.

Before we get into this too much though, you need to understand that the limited partnership, limited liability company, and the corporation balance sheets are going to be a lot different from the regular household balance sheet. This is mainly because these companies have a lot of complex items in their accounting records to keep the company going. This is why many of these companies rely on an accountant to help them get it done.

Businesses are often faced with many difficult questions that others may not know the answers to, such as how to depreciate out the costs for some of their business expenses, how to record the lease obligations, how to account for the expenses of construction at the power plan, and so much more.

No matter how overwhelming it can seem in the beginning to figure out all the different parts of the balance sheet, it is actually pretty simple once you have looked at a few. The best way to get through the balance sheet is to remember that the purpose of this financial statement is to answer three basic questions for anyone who is looking at that sheet. These three main questions that the balance sheet should answer include:

What does the company have? These will be the assets of the company.

What does the company owe on? These will be the liabilities of the company.

What is left over for the owners of that business if they were to pay off all their debts? This one is going to be the shareholder equity or the book value.

These are pretty advanced terms and fancy words, but they are there to help give the investor a good idea of where the business is at that time. If you can remember the objective of the balance sheet, all those fancy words and accounting complexities won't seem as overwhelming when you take a look over it later.

One thing to remember is that unlike some of the other financial statements, the balance sheet is not going to cover a range of dates. The information that is present in the balance sheet is going to be good as of the date that is on the balance sheet, but it won't be able to tell you any date ranges in the process. If you are looking to deal with this issue when calculating many of the accounting ratios, then the best way to do this is to work with the averagely weighted figures of the balance sheet.

An example of this is if you would like to figure out what the average value of inventory was for that year for the company. You would be able to do this by taking the value of the inventory at the previous yearend, add it to the inventory's value at the end of this year, and then divide them by two.

This is a fast trick that will help you to avoid any distortions by ending period figures that may or may not be able to reflect what occurred throughout that year accurately. For example, if the manufacturing business was able to pay off all the debt it had in the year, and this showed that there was $0 in liabilities on this balance sheet, but then there was a line there to show the interest expense on your income statement, this could be confusing.

By taking the time to weigh the average debt outstanding from the balance sheet over that same period, you may be able to get a better idea of what the business has going on here and why they listed some interest costs on the income statement but not on the balance sheet.

What Are the Different Types of Assets?

Next, we need to take a look at some of the assets that the company needs to keep track of. Remember that these assets are going to help the company do its normal operations. There are two types of assets that each business will need to pay attention to, including current assets and noncurrent assets.

Current Assets

Current assets are going to be any that the company owns that have a lifespan that is a year or less. This means that the asset has to be easily changed over to cash if the company needs to. Such assets will include inventory, accounts receivable, and cash or cash equivalents.

Cash, which is the most fundamental and most commonly thought about the current asset, can also include checks and bank accounts that are not restricted. Cash equivalents are going to be assets that are very safe, but which can also be turned into cash quickly if the company needs. The US Treasury is a good example of this. And then there are the accounts receivables, which are going to show the reader any of the obligations that customers and others owe to the company over the short-term. These sometimes happen if a company allows the customer to use credit to purchase the product or service.

Inventory is an important current asset as well. Inventory can include things like the raw materials to make a product, the products that are still in the process of being created, and the finished goods. Each company is going to be different, and the exact way that the inventory account looks is going to be different. For a manufacturing firm, there may be a lot of raw materials, but a retained firm wouldn't have any raw materials.

Noncurrent Assets

These noncurrent assets are going to be any that you are not able to turn into cash very easily, which the company doesn't plan to turn into cash soon. These also include items that will last more than a year. Tangible assets such as land and buildings are included in this. Sometimes, the intangible items will be added to this as well.

What Are the Different Liabilities?

Another part of the balance sheet is the liabilities. These are going to be any financial obligations that the company owes to an outside party. Similar to the assets above, these will fall under the idea of being either a current liability or one that will last long-term.

The long-term liabilities are going to be any of the debts that the company has that will be due in more than a year from that balance sheet date. The current liabilities though are going to be any liabilities that need to be paid off within a year. This could include some of the shorter-term borrowings or even the latest interest that you paid on a longer loan.

The company needs to properly list out all the liabilities that they have on this balance sheet. This helps the investor or the lender know how many debts and obligations that the company is dealing with, and then they can compare this to the profits of the company to see where the company stands financially. This information is much more important to making sound decisions for the investor or the lender compared to just looking at the profits.

For example, a company may have some great profits, but if they have such high debts that they can barely keep up with them, then those high profits don't mean anything. The investors and lenders want to make sure that the company is able to handle their debts and pay them off, while still making a profit and paying their investors before they put any money into it.

Shareholders' Equity

The shareholder's equity is going to be the beginning amount of money that the owners and others put into the business. If at the end of that year, the company wants to take their net earnings and reinvest it back into the company, then these earnings need to move over to your income statement and then placed into the equity account for the shareholder to make it work. This account is important because it will represent the net worth of the company.

The balance sheet is so important to a business. It gives a great snapshot of the finances of a business and can give analysts, investors, and lenders a good idea of where the business stands financially.

Filling it out properly is going to make a big difference in how people view your company.

The Cash Flow Statement

The third document that needs to be found in the financial report of a business is the cash flow statement. This is going to be an important financial statement because it will showcase the amount of cash and cash equivalents that will enter or leave that company. This statement can also measure how well the company can manage its cash position. This means that it shows the capability of the company to earn money or cash and then put that money toward all the debts and other obligations that are needed to fund any expenses to keep the business going.

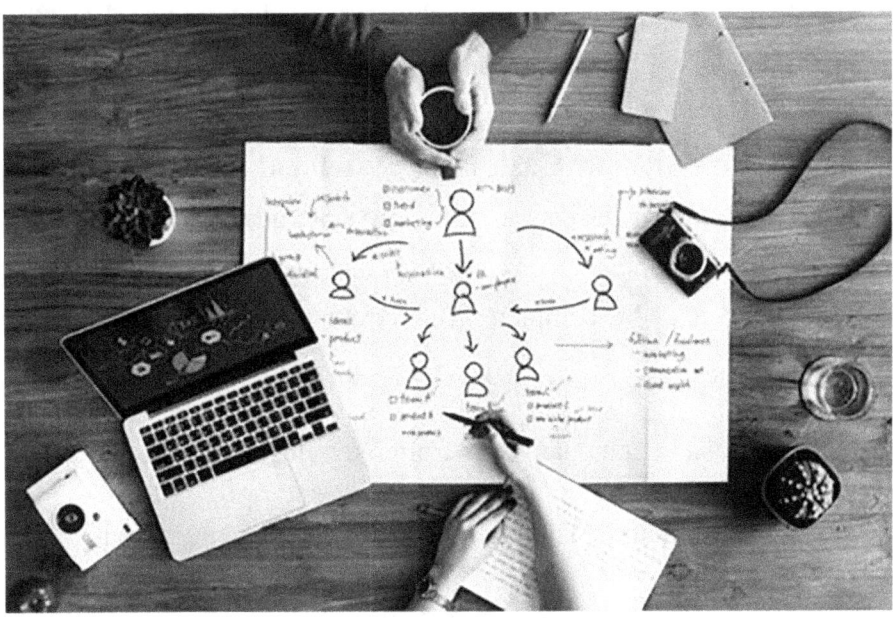

This statement will help finish out the financial statements of the company, along with the income statement and the balance sheet, and it is mandatory that all three of these documents are presented.

What ways can I use this statement?

There are many reasons that this statement can help out a business. First, the cash flow statement is there to help any investor to understand how well the company is running its operations. It can also explain where the company is getting its money from and how they are spending that money. The cash flow statement is so important because it can be used to help investors determine how financially secure the company is at that time and whether it is a smart decision to invest with them.

Investors, as well as many creditors, will use the cash flow statement to help determine how much cash is available. This is referred to as the liquidity of the company. This cash needs to be used to help the company fund any operating expenses that it has and pay off its debts.

The Structure of Your Cash Flow Statement

When an accountant designs a cash flow statement for any business, there are some components or categories that need to be present in this document for it to be complete. These four components include the following:

- Any cash the company gets from operating activities.

- Any cash that the company gets from its investing activities.

- Any cash that the company gets from financing activities.

- This category includes any activities that are noncash. These are sometimes included, and it will depend on the rules found under GAAP, or the generally accepted accounting principles.

Of note here is that the cash flow statement is going to be different from the other financial documents that we talked about before. The main reason is that the cash flow statement is not going to have information about all cash that may happen in the future that is recorded as a credit. Because of this, cash is not going to be considered the same thing as net income.

Operating Activities

Now we need to break down the components of the cash flow statement so we know what needs to go into each part. The operating activities will be first. These operating activities found on the cash flow statement will be any sources as well as uses of cash from the business activities of that company. To make it easy, this is going to reflect how much cash that company is able to generate through doing business or offering their products and services to the customer.

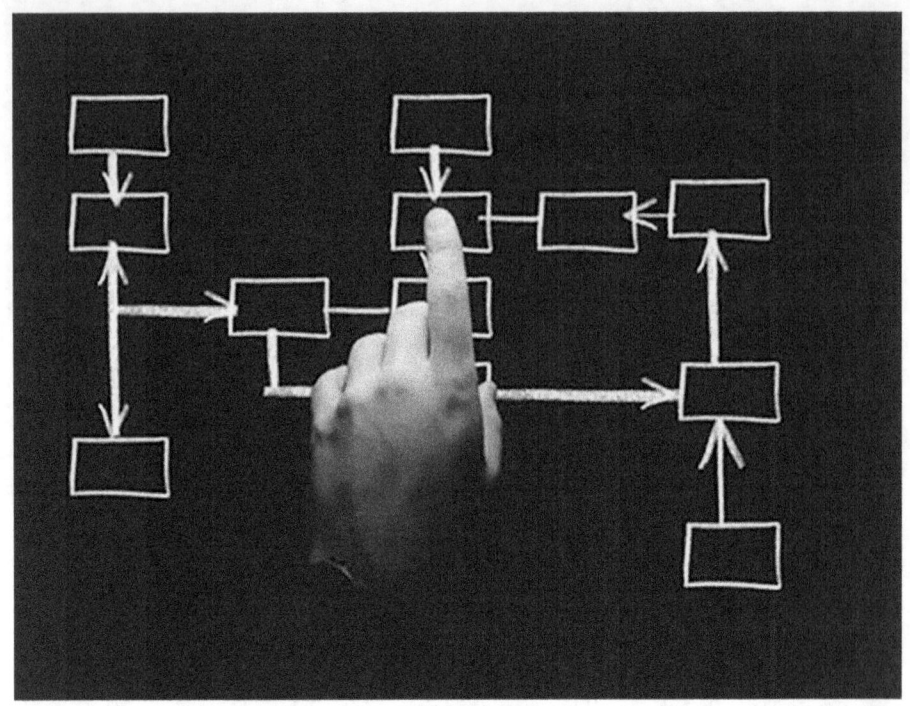

Generally, any of the changes that the company makes in cash, depreciation, accounts payable, inventory, and accounts receivable can be reflected in cash from operations. Some examples of the operating activities of the company would include:

- Any payments for rent

- The payments you make for wages and salary to the employees.

- Payments that you make for suppliers for the services and goods that you use in production.

- Any tax payments you make on income.

- Any interest payments you make on loans or your mortgage.

- Receipts from any sales of the services or goods you sell.

When it comes to the trading portfolio, or if it is an investment company, it would have receipts about debt or equity instruments, and receipts from the sale of a loan can be included. When you try to prepare this cash flow statement under the indirect method (we will talk about this method in a bit), things like deferred tax, any losses or gains that the company may get from assets that are noncurrent, amortization, depreciation, and dividends that come from the investment opportunities of the company and more can be included. However, with this indirect method, purchase, or any sales of your long-term assets can't be counted under the operating activities.

How Can I Calculate My Cash Flow?

Now we need to learn how to calculate the cash flow of a company. The cash flow is going to be calculated simply by making certain adjustments to the net income for that company. You can do this by either subtracting or adding the differences in credit transactions, expenses, and revenue that come from any transaction that will occur between two accounting periods. The numbers that you will use are found on several of the financial documents to help you get started.

These adjustments need to be made because there are some noncash items that have been calculated into the net income (found on the income statement) as well as into the liabilities and the total assets found on the balance sheet. So since not all your transactions are going to involve some actual cash items, then you need to re-evaluate some of the items to come up with an accurate number for cash flow from operations.

Because you have to go through and make some changes to get an accurate number, there are going to be two main methods that accountants can use to make sure that you are able to come up with the cash flow numbers. The two main methods are the direct and then the indirect method.

With the direct method, you are going to get all your cash payments and receipts and add them up. This information can include cash that you paid to suppliers, cash that you paid to your employees for salaries and cash receipts from the customer. These figures are going to be calculated by using the end and the beginning balances from your different business accounts, and then you can check whether there is an increase or a decrease in the net amounts of these accounts.

You can also choose to work with the indirect method. In this method, the cash flow from all your operating activities will be calculated. You will first take the net income off the income statement because this income statement for the company will be prepared on what is known as an accrual basis. When you use this method, the revenue for that company is only recognized at the time of earnings rather than at the time it is received.

Because of this information, the net income is not always the best representation of how the company's cash flow is doing. This is why you will need to go through and make some adjustments for any of the items that will affect your net income. Yes, the company is still waiting to receive cash for the product or service, but it still needs adjustment.

With the indirect method, you will also need to make adjustments to make sure that some of your nonoperating activities are added back in. An example of doing this would be with depreciation. Since this depreciation of assets is not seen in most cases as a cash expense, it needs to be added back in with the total you receive on the net sales during that cash flow calculation. You only want to add this asset into your statement when it is time to sell it.

The amount that the accounts receivable decreases is then going to be added into the net sales is how many customers paid off their credit accounts that period, and that number needs to be added to the net sales of the company.

But if there is an increase between one period of accounting to another in the accounts receivable, then the amount needs to be deducted from your net sales. Even though the amounts are counted as revenue in the accounts receivable, they are not really cash, so it shouldn't show up on the cash flow statement.

The change in inventory is also another thing to go through and check on. When the company has an increase in the amount of inventory they have, it could signal that the company spent more of their money to purchase the raw materials that they need to make the products. If the inventory was paid off with cash, then the increase in this inventory needs to be taken from your net sales. A decrease in the amount of inventory that you have is added over to the net sales part of the statement. If you ended up purchasing some inventory and did so on credit, then you need to see an increase in the accounts payable section. Then you need to have the increased amount from the past year put in with the net sales.

This same process is going to work with other parts of your company as well. It could work for prepaid insurance, salaries payable, taxes payable, and more. If you pay something off, then you will subtract the difference in value that you owed from one year to the following one from the net income. But if you still have some that are owed on that item, then this difference needs to be added to the net earnings.

The Investing Activities and Your Cash Flow Statement

Some of the investing activities that the company partakes in can be used on the cash flow statement as well. Investing activities can be any source or any use of the cash from any investments the company participates in. These may include things like purchasing a new asset, loans that are made to a vendor, a loan that is received from customers, or any payments that the company receives because of an acquisition or a merger. In short, any changes that occur from investments, assets, or equipment will relate to the cash you have from investing.

In most cases, any changes in cash because of your investments are just going to end with a cash out of the item, mostly because you took that cash and used it to purchase buildings, new equipment, or even some shorter-term assets, like a marketable security. However, if your company decides to divest an asset, then this transaction is going to be called cash in for helping you calculate your cash from investing.

Financing Activities and Your Cash Flow Statement

Cash that comes from the financing activities on your cash flow statement will include the sources of cash from investors or bank, and it can also include uses of cash that you paid out to the shareholders. Payments for repurchasing stocks, payment for dividends, and repayment of debts or loans can all be added to this category.

If you have some changes in cash from this financing, then you are cashing in whenever the capital rises, but then cashed out when the dividends are paid. So if a company issues out a bond to the public, then the company will receive some cash for that financing. However, when they have to pay out some interest to the bondholders, the company will reduce the amount of cash that it has control over at that time.

Tying Together the Income Statement, the Balance Sheet, and the Cash Flow Statement

As we mentioned earlier, the cash flow statement is going to rely on the balance sheet and the income statement to come up with the numbers that you will use in your calculations. Changes are needed to the numbers to get an accurate value, but if you filled out your balance sheet and your income statement properly, then you will have the information that you need to start on the cash flow statement.

Net earnings that are found in the income statement will be used as the figure for the cash flow statement. Without this information, or with the wrong information, then the information is going to show up wrong on the cash flow statement as well.

In regard to this balance sheet, your net cash flow is going to be measurable as well. If the cash decreased or increased between your balance sheets, then the net cash flow needs to change the same amount, or something is wrong. So if you are trying to come up with the cash flow for 2017, then you would use all the balance sheets from 2016 to 2017 to help you get the right information.

The cash flow statement is an important document, which is why it is included along with the other financial documents for a company. This statement is going to measure the strength, the profitability, and the outlook over the long-term for the company. The cash flow statement helps an investor, a manager, and others determine whether the company has enough cash and that the cash is liquid enough to pay off its expenses. A company can often rely on this cash flow statement to predict how their cash flow might be at a future time, which can be so important when they are working on things like budgeting for the future of that company.

For investors, the cash flow statement is a major tool that investors and managers like to work with. Since the cash flow statement is going to reflect the financial health of the company, since it is typical that when a company has more cash, then the better off they are doing. However, there are some times when this rule doesn't really work for the business. For example, there are times when a company will have a negative cash flow because of the growth strategy they chose. If the company expands its operations, it may eliminate some of its cash flow, but it will quickly gain those back and more once the operations are up and running.

When an investor takes the time to study the cash flow statement, the investor is going to get one of the best pictures of how much cash the company is able to generate. They get a good understanding of how financially secure the company is at that time. And it can help them to choose whether or not they want to invest in that company.

Tax Accounting

No matter the type of business you run, there will come a time when you need to file your taxes. In your first year, you may not need to do this as you get things organized and up and running. But after that, or once you owe $1000 or more to the IRS if you are a sole proprietorship, then you will need to pay your taxes each quarter.

Having accurate records and filling out the income statement, the balance sheet, and the cash flow statement can make it easier to do your taxes. You can just insert the numbers into your tax forms, and you can use this information to help you get the deductions to save you even more.

With the help of your accountant, you will be able to take all the documents that you have and get your tax documents all set up and ready. Let's take a look at tax accounting, how it works, and why it is so important to your business to get this done.

What Is Tax Accounting?

Tax accounting is a subset of accounting. It is going to focus on preparing and handling taxes rather than the public financial statements of the company. Tax accounting is going to be governed by the Internal Revenue Code, which will dictate the specific rules that all individuals and companies need to follow when they work on their tax returns.

Tax accounting is a basic means of accounting to help get taxes done. It can actually apply to everyone, including corporations, business, individuals, and other entities. Even those who have exemptions for paying taxes need to do some tax accounting. The purpose of this kind of accounting is to be able to track the funds of the company, including those that go out and those that come in, associated with entities and with individuals.

Having proof of all this information can be really helpful at tax time. Even if your income was small enough, or you had enough deductions or both not to pay taxes, it is going to be helpful to have a record of all the funds coming in and out of your business. You can keep track of your business progress and can prove your income if you are ever audited in the future.

The Tax Principles vs. GAAP

If you own a business or do accounting in the United States, you will notice that there are going to be two core sets of principles that can be used. These two rules are different, and you should not confuse them. The first is going to be principles that are used specifically in tax accounting, and the second ones will be for a financial account in general.

Under the rules of GAAP, all companies will need to follow a common set of procedures, standards, and principles in their accounting any time that they compile a financial statement and with all their financial transactions. The GAAP rules will list out all the rules that you need to follow in order to write your balance sheets, income statement, and cash flow statement. There are various different rules that you will need to follow with GAAP, and it ensures that companies are going to record their financial information and that there is some unity between the financial statements.

While accounting is going to have a little bit to do with all the financial transactions, tax accounting is going to focus all its energy on transactions that will affect the tax burden of a company, and how those items will relate to proper tax calculations and preparation with tax documents.

Tax accounting has some regulations placed on it and is regulated by the IRS to make sure that all the tax laws are followed by individual taxpayers and tax accounting professionals. The IRS is also going to use specific documents and forms so that you can submit the tax information properly as the law requires from you.

Tax Accounting and How It Works for an Individual

Tax accounting can work for both individuals and for businesses. First, we are going to look at tax accounting and how it works for an individual. As an individual who pays taxes, tax accounting is going to focus mostly on items like the income of the individual, the deductions that they qualify for, any investments that they earned or lost on, and some other transactions that will affect how much you pay taxes.

This is good because it is going to help limit the amount of information that individuals need to manage to finish their tax return. You don't have to go through and keep receipts of every transaction that you make for example. If you make a big purchase, you keep that receipt, but a grocery store trip isn't one that you need to keep track of at all. This makes it easier for most individuals to get their tax returns done without all the work.

With general accounting, the individual would have to go through a lot more work. General accounting would mean that you need to track all the funds that come in and then go out of the person's possession, no matter what the purpose. If you got some clothes, you would have to write that on the tax return. If you went out to eat, you would have to write that out as well. You would have to write out everything that is a personal expense even if those expenses had no tax implications.

With tax accounting, you only have to keep track of a few things for the year. You keep track of any income that you make either from investments, from a job or other sources. And then you keep track of the items that can be deducted from your taxes to reduce your tax burden. And then that is it.

Tax Accounting for a Business

Businesses are often going to benefit the most from tax accounting. Tax accounting is going to help a business to keep track of everything that it needs to use for tax purposes. It can also help them to get as many tax deductions as possible in order to save them money.

From the perspective of a business, more information needs to be analyzed to finish the process for tax accounting. While the company needs to track its incoming funds and earnings, similar to what the individual has to do, there is also another level of complexity that comes with business tax accounting. This comes with outgoing funds that are directed toward the obligations of the business.

There are a lot of different parts that the business needs to keep track of for tax accounting. This sometimes includes funds that are directed toward specific expenses of the business, or the funds that are directed out to the shareholders of the business.

While a business doesn't have to use a tax accountant to do these duties, many larger organizations will have one. Tax accounting is going to be pretty complex. The larger your business is, the more complex the tax accounting process will be and having a tax accountant can help make this easier.

How Tax Accounting Works for Organizations Exempt from Taxes

There are some entities or businesses that are going to be exempt from taxes. Even in these instances, the business will need to perform tax accounting. This is mainly due to the fact that all businesses need to file an annual term. This is true no matter how much they owe in taxes and even if they are tax-exempt for the year.

These businesses will need to provide information that is in regard to their incoming funds, such as any donations or grants that the business gets. They will then need to explain how they will use these funds to help them operate during the year.

The point of doing this is to ensure that these businesses are following all the regulations and laws that govern the way that a tax-exempt business can run and operate. Even though these businesses will not end up having to pay any taxes, regardless of how much they make during the year, it is important to fill out the return and keep track of the information. This can show the IRS that you are using all your funds properly.

Tax accounting can be a difficult part to work on. There are a lot of rules and regulations that a business must adhere to and making sure that everything is filed right with the IRS is important. Hiring a tax accountant can make it easier to get this done without running into trouble at the end of the year.

What's New in Bookkeeping for Small Business?

Bookkeeping is always changing, and new software is always coming out. Let's look at some of these techniques and software programs that are out there for you to use as a small business owner.

Open a Business Bank Account

You want to see your business succeed. However, how do you keep your personal finances separate from your business finances? The answer is simple; just open a business bank account.

It is extremely hard to see how your business is doing if you combine your business revenue and expenses with your personal. The best way is to check with your bank first to see if they have a business account available.

Using a spreadsheet is basic. Although, what if your business has inventory, employees, vendors, etc.? This is when an accounting or bookkeeping software could come in handy. My recommendation is QuickBooks or Xero as they both provide for these types of accounts.

Choose the Best Bookkeeping Software for your Business

Choosing a software can vary based on your needs. At the minimum, you will need a ledger or cashbook. The cashbook that would include the general journal and the ledges can easily be done using a spreadsheet like Microsoft Excel or Google Sheets. Remember, Google Sheet will allow you to save it through Google and have access to the file anywhere you are.

QuickBooks and Xero may not be the best for your business. Sometimes, the most difficult part is finding the software that works best for your needs.

Let's look at a few different bookkeeping applications that may get you started. I will include QuickBooks and Xero.

Intuit QuickBooks Online

QuickBooks Online is by far the best accounting and bookkeeping software for small businesses. I like that you can link it to your bank account. This makes it easy to use and track money when linked to your business account. It makes it easy to reconcile the business account and the books. Although there is so much more to QuickBooks Online.

Just a few of the features within QuickBooks Online include:

- Invoicing

- Expense Tracking

- Inventory Management

- Purchase Ordering

- Reporting

As your business grows, you can upgrade your account between the top three tiers. This will allow you to have everything you need for your small business. Another part that is great about QuickBooks Online is that there are apps for your phone both through Android and iOS devices. The software is also compatible with most third-party applications.

QuickBooks Online also offers some of the best pricing. There are four tiers of pricing, depending on what you need for your business. It also offers a thirty-day free trial. However, if you want to just jump right into it and go for the paid versions, you will get a 50% discount for the first six months. That means if you are just starting your business you will have six months to make a little extra profit and get established before you need to pay full price.

The most basic is the self-employed plan. This plan is $10 per month. It is designed for independent contractors and freelancers. It allows the following:

- Track Mileage

- Track Income and Expenses

- Create Invoices

- Accept Payments

- Run Reports

Keep in mind the self-employed plan cannot be upgraded to a higher tier. It will require you to create and set up a new account.

The next tier is the Simple Start plan. With this plan, a single user is supported and costs $15 per month. This plan includes the following:

- Track Mileage

- Track Income and Expenses

- Create Invoices

- Accept Payments

- Run Reports

- Send Estimates

- Track Sales and Sales Tax

The next tier is the Essentials plan. This plan supports multiple users and costs $35 per month. This plan includes the following:

- Track Mileage

- Track Income and Expenses

- Create Invoices

- Accept Payments

- Run Reports

- Send Estimates

- Track Sales and Sales Tax

- Bill Management

- Time Tracking

The last tier is the Plus plan. This plan also allows for multiple users and costs $50 per month. This plan includes the following:

- Track Mileage

- Track Income and Expenses

- Create Invoices

- Accept Payments

- Run Reports

- Send Estimates

- Track Sales and Sales Tax

- Bill Management

- Time Tracking

- Track Inventory

- Create Budgets

- Pay Independent Contractors that use the 1099 form

Like most small business, you will eventually have employees that you will need to pay. With QuickBooks Online, you can add this feature to any of the top three tiers for an additional monthly cost.

The best part is QuickBooks Online is very user-friendly. This software also has a good timesaving feature that you need in any good accounting and bookkeeping program. It will keep track of due dates for invoices, sync your business bank account, track your credit card transactions, and so much more. This allows you to focus more time on the business and less time on the books while maintaining accurate bookkeeping throughout your business and giving you a great outlook of the financials of the business. Another good timesaving feature that puts QuickBooks Online on top is that you can send out invoices to customers, allowing them to pay online at a click of a button.

Like with any application, things tend to go wrong with the program itself. That is why QuickBooks Online offers both phone and chat support. You can access this from the company website making it easier and quicker to get issues resolved and have you up and running again without missing a sale.

QuickBooks Online is account approved. This means that no matter what your needs are you can give your accountant access to your books. Remember, that your account will not take up a spot in your users that you give access to.

Like all programs, there are some limitations, although with QuickBooks Online it seems like the sky is the limit. The limitations really lay within mobile apps. Here are the things you can do with mobile apps:

- Send invoices.

- Reconcile transactions.

- Take photos of receipts and attach to expenses.

- View customer information and add new customers.

- View dashboard data, such as account balance, profit and loss reports, and open and past due invoices.

After looking through what the app can do, if you feel like that works perfect, then QuickBooks Online is the perfect software for you. However, if you prefer doing most of your accounting and bookkeeping through your phone, then there is another accounting and bookkeeping software choice for you.

Xero

If you would rather use a PC or a Mac, Xero has a lot to offer. Xero is by far the best accounting and bookkeeping software for Mac users. It easy to use and learn. What I like about Xero are the videos. Everything you do in Xero will have a video that will help you learn the software.

Xero also has comparable prices and is listed into three different plans. The starter plan is $9 per month. It does have some limitations. These are the features of the starter plan:

- Unlimited Users

- Limit to Five Invoices per month

- Limit to Five Bills per month

- Limit to 20 Transaction Reconciliations per month

The standard plan is $30 per month. This includes:

- Unlimited Users

- Unlimited Invoices

- Unlimited Bills

- Unlimited Transaction Reconciliations

- Payroll for up to Five Employees

The premium plan is $70 per month. Which includes:

- Unlimited Users

- Unlimited Invoices

- Unlimited Bills

- Unlimited Transaction Reconciliations

- Payroll for up to 10 Employees. Note: this can be adjusted to support more employees if needed.

- Supports Multiple Currencies. Note: this is a great feature if you do international business.

The best part is that there are not any long-term contracts for using Xero. That means you can change at any time without having additional fees. There is also a free 30-day trial to let you try and find out if it will be the best for your business.

Much like QuickBooks Online, Xero also has many timesaving features. You can send out invoices electronically, which also allows for your customers to pay online easily. You can also turn quotes and estimates into invoices with only a few clicks. This allows for you to give a customer a quote and if they agree to go with your services you can turn that quote into an invoice and get paid.

With your business bank account linked to Xero, the system will allow you to set scheduled payments and manually pay the bills. This helps save time and ensures that all bills are paid on time and you do not need to worry about past-dues and late fees.

If you need to claim an expense that occurred, then Xero will help you to record, manage, claim, and reimburse the expense claims. You can also add expenses easily and attach the receipt images.

Xero has some great inventory management tools available for small businesses that do not offer services and instead sell merchandises that are kept in inventory. Here you can track your inventory and show how much inventory you have in stock.

As I mentioned with QuickBooks Online, it has limitations when it comes to mobile apps. Xero is one of these programs that allows for great mobile accessibility. The mobile app for Xero allows you to do the following:

- Create and send invoices

- Add receipts

- Attach billable expenses to customer invoices

- Submit expense reports

- Reconcile transactions

- Access your dashboard for a real-time view of your cash flow

- Use an additional app for employees for submitting time sheets, request time off, and view paystubs

One thing that sets Xero apart from other software is that it also has the capability to have a developer design and customize your own app by providing the API to allow for integration to your Xero account.

There is also a 24-7 customer support for those times that you have issues with your account, allowing you to have your books back up without losing the sale. However, there is one drawback to Xero. There are not many accountant and bookkeepers who know the software. Therefore, it brings in limitations to finding someone to keep your books.

Zoho Books

If you are a sole proprietor, freelancer or E-Commerce with a home-based business, then this is a great bookkeeping software for you. It is easy to use and affordable. It will allow you to connect with all your accounts and it covers all the basic needs of your business.

Zoho Books offer three pricing plans. The basic plan is $9 per month. This plan only supports one user and allows you to add 50 contacts. Other features include the following:

- Reconcile Transactions

- Create Invoices

- Track Expenses

- Manage Projects

- Manage Time Sheets

The standard plan is $19 per month and supports two users. It also allows for 500 contacts to be added. This plan includes the following:

- Reconcile Transactions

- Create Invoices

- Track Expenses

- Manage Projects

- Manage Time Sheets

- Track Bills

- Track Vendor Credits

- Add Reporting Tags to your Transactions

The professional plan is $29 per month and allows for ten users. This plan also allows for unlimited contacts. It also includes the following:

- Reconcile Transactions

- Create Invoices

- Track Expenses

- Manage Projects

- Manage Time Sheets

- Track Bills

- Track Vendor Credits

- Add Reporting Tags to your Transactions

- Create Sales Orders

- Create Purchase Orders

- Manage Inventory

Zoho Books has one of the best customer services and support. The phones are open 24 hours a day, five days a week.

One disadvantage of Zoho Books is that it does not offer payroll services. If you have employees, then you would need software that is for payroll. If you do not have employees, then this is the best for you and your business.

FreshBooks

I mentioned earlier that there is software for bookkeeping that is great for those who want more accessibility through mobile apps. What makes FreshBooks the best is that you can find almost all the features in the mobile app that you have on the website. Keep in mind that if your business has inventory, then this may not be the software for you.

Most all the software we have been talking about is based on features. With FreshBooks, the pricing is based on active clients. For the Lite plan, it is $15 per month and allows you to bill up to five clients. The plus plan is $25 per month and allows you to bill up 50 clients. The premium plan is $50 and allows to bill up to 500 clients.

For each of the plans, you can add contractors at no additional cost. However, if you need to add employees, it is an extra $10 per month for each employee. Contractors and employees can view different parts of the books.

Employees can do the following:

- View and create invoices and expenses

- View the dashboard

- Generate reports

- Contractors can:

- View projects they have been assigned to

- Track time toward the assigned projects

- Create and send you invoices for their time

FreshBooks also has some timesaving features. You can create, send and manage invoices easily. This can be done from your computer or mobile app. It also allows for faster payments and makes tracking your expenses easy and allows for project management and time tracking.

With all software, customer service is a must. You will find both phone and email support. However, it is not 24-7 support. They do have hours between 8:00 a.m. to 8:00 p.m. Eastern Standard Time Monday through Friday. With such a great interface of the mobile app, then they also have support for those issues that may arise as well.

Wave Accounting

That brings us to the last bookkeeping software we are going to look at, Wave Accounting. Wave Accounting is great if you do not have much equity to start with, as this software is free. Yes, that's right, I did say free.

Wave Accounting is designed for very small businesses with ten employees or fewer and no inventory. If your business offers services, then you may want to try it out. If you plan on growing your business, eventually you will need to transition to another form of software.

Keep in mind, what keeps Wave Accounting free is the use of advertising. That means it will not only post advertising on the software while you use it, but it will also include its branding on your communications with customers.

You can also add credit card processing for a small fee per transaction. The same goes for payroll processing as this can be added for $15 per month as well as an additional $4 per employee per month.

Keep in mind that Wave Accounting does still offer the basics for the needs of your company. With the advertising, if you want to have your business separated from all the ads, then you may want to choose a different software such as Zoho Books.

Create a Logo

One thing that will set your business apart from the rest is the business logo you create. This logo will be displayed on invoices, business cards, brochures, website, etc.

This should represent your business. You don't have to spend a lot of money on a good design. Search around, and you will find a lot of sites that offer logo design for cheaper.

If you have some creative talent and want to create your own, you can do that as well. A great place to start is through https://www.canva.com. This site is user-friendly and free, although you do not need to use this site. You can easily create it in Word, Photoshop, Paint, etc. Make sure to save your logo as a JPG or PNG. If you use Word, then hit print screen and copy it into Paint so that you can save it in the proper format. Chose a good size for the logo and crop if needed. You may want to save different sizes as well. For example, you may have one size for your invoices, a size for your business cards, and a size for your letterhead when sending out emails and letters on behalf of the business.

Monthly Bookkeeping Reports

Many times, businesses start to struggle because they do not know how the business is doing from the beginning. A good rule of thumb is to actively have the books up-to-date and always accurate. This will help when you do reports.

Also, make sure you are pulling the reports monthly. Do not just wait until the end of the quarter or year. If you have the reports each month it will give you a better understanding of how your business is doing and can help you make changes, if needed, for the following month.

With that said, I also want you to understand it is also just as important to do quarterly and yearly reports. This will help you judge how the business is doing overall throughout the year and throughout the years.

Hire Employees

Adding employees to your business is not always the easiest to keep up with. It brings new responsibilities as you will need to keep track and pay their wages. One thing that can help with this is the bookkeeping software applications that we have discussed. It is worth ensuring you have the payroll feature if you have employees. Your employees rely on this paycheck.

Granted with payroll, you also have payroll taxes. This money belongs to the government. One thing that could help with this is to have a separate savings account within your business account for holding all the payroll taxes. That way, when it comes time to pay the government, the money is already set aside.

Make sure you are filing the correct documents for payroll on time; otherwise, you could encounter added fines.

Try New Systems

There are so many systems out there that will help your business succeed. We have talked about a few of the software programs used for bookkeeping. However, if you add too many systems at once it could be overwhelming for you, your employees, and your customers.

As the business owner, you need to select carefully the applications you need for your business. A good rule of thumb is to only try the systems that are needed for either maintenance or growth. If your business does not need it for either one of these, then do not add them! One thing that could help with this is having a website or mobile app designed that integrates everything you need for your business. You can add a feature that allows you, your employees, and your customers to access the same app, but based on their credentials they will only have access to what is needed for them.

Keep in mind, if you introduce one system at a time, you will be able to give everyone a chance to learn the system before introducing the next.

Be Hands-on with Your Bookkeeper

As a business owner, you need to take a hands-on approach with your bookkeeper. In the starting phase, you might not afford to hire a bookkeeper and therefore must do it yourself or have one of your staff members do it. Always make sure you know what is going on with your accounts if you allow your staff to do the bookkeeping.

Bookkeeping is basic transactions, but you do need to see those reports each month, quarter, and year. If you record an invoice or expense in the wrong account, the books can still, balance but the accounts may not.

A bookkeeper needs to know and understand where all transactions will be recorded. I would also say the same about the business owner. If you are the business owner, you need to read the reports each month and know if something does not look right and needs to be reviewed. The same goes for the bookkeeper. If you are the bookkeeper, you need to go through all the transactions that were recorded that month to ensure that they were recorded in the correct account before the reports are generated.

One thing you could do is have a professional consultant bookkeeper look at the books for any errors. If you are worried about upsetting your bookkeeper, then add it to your company policy that a routine audit will be conducted at the end of each month or quarter.

Outsource to a Bookkeeper

If you, as the business owner, is also the bookkeeper for an extended period of time, then you may want to outsource your bookkeeping. This can be the most cost effective as you are only paying for a couple of hours of work. On the other hand, if you had an employee assigned to it, you are paying a monthly wage. You can also outsource to ensure that the books are being handled by a professional and will be accurate.

In general, it could take a professional bookkeeper only two to four hours to process an entire month of transactions and provide your business with the monthly reports you require.

If you feel that you can handle some of the bookkeeping and only want the professional to handle specific areas you can do that as well.

One of the benefits of outsourcing to a professional is that they can give great business advice that will help your business grow. Some of this advice could be, but is not limited to the following:

- New software and if they would be a good fit for your business

- Attend business meetings with you and your banker

- Help with annual budget and cash flow reports

- Train office employees

Understanding How Taxes Work
for Your Small Business

In addition to helping you keep track of the financial information for your business, doing well with your bookkeeping can help you get prepared when it is time for tax season. Many new business owners feel a bit overwhelmed when it is time to do their taxes. But if you have maintained your books through the year, then tax time is going to be easy.

There are a few things that you need to know before filing your federal income tax. As a small business, you may make the mistake of thinking the IRS is not concerned with your tax liability. However, the IRS does care quite a bit. This chapter will take a look at some of the things that you should watch out for when it comes to working on your taxes.

The Legal Entity You Choose Can Affect Your Tax Burden

Your small business may not have to shoulder the same tax burden that another one does. The legal entity that you go with can have a bit effect on the amount of tax liability that you have throughout the years.

There are different types of entities that your business can choose. You can be a sole proprietorship, an LLC or an S corporation to name a few. The S corporation is beneficial because it allowed you the advantage of being able to pay your taxes at the same level as a shareholder, but it does limit how many stocks you can use. The C Corporation can help you deduct more expenses at tax time, but it includes double taxation and a lot more paperwork compared to others.

You should carefully look through your business and decide which of these entities is the best one for your needs. Each one has a benefit and some negatives, so you want to look through them all to make sure that you pick out the best one for your needs.

You Can Sometimes Deduct More than You Think

As a small business, you are probably used to having to stretch out your budget as far as possible. You may not have the stockholders to rely on, and you certainly don't have the large budget that some of the capital that the bigger companies should have. Despite this smaller business budget, you still need to pay for raw materials, rent for the building you use, the salaries of any employees you hire, the operational costs, and even utilities. The good news is that a small business owner is able to deduct many of these expenses and lower their tax burdens so they can stretch their business profits further.

According to information from the IRS, a business is able to deduct any expense that is deemed necessary and ordinary for that industry. These ordinary expenses are going to be any of those that are common for your specific trade. Necessary expenses are the ones that make your work easier but aren't necessarily used by every business.

There are a lot of expenses that can fall into this and that you are able to deduct when it is tax season. You can deduct the rent in your home office or business, computers, office equipment, supplies, and more. In addition, small businesses can deduct the costs that they pay when providing healthcare benefits to any employees. You should take the time to research all the deductions that apply to you to help save money and lessen your tax bill.

It is important that you go through all the deductions and see if they pertain to you. This is one of the best ways to help you save money on the amount that you pay in taxes. You can then put this money back into your business and see it grow some more.

Remember Those Startup Expenses

One mistake that a new startup will make is thinking that the expenses they incur for starting a business can't be deducted. However, the IRS will allow small business owners to deduct quite a few of their startup expenses, even the ones that occur before they open their doors.

Although the expenses for starting up a business will differ depending on the industry, most businesses could deduct any investigational costs they incur when analyzing products and researching the market for their product. You can deduce costs for training employees, going to trade shows, locating suppliers, and even advertising to your potential employees.

One thing to note here is that you can only deduct the expenses that lead to the creation of a viable business entity. If you decide, after going through these expenses, not to form the business, then these costs become personal expenses, and it is possible that none of them will be deductible.

If you want to claim some of the expenses that you incurred while opening the business, you must keep good records ahead of time. This will make it easier to prove these expenses at tax time. If you keep them all organized through the year, it will also save you time having to search through everything later to find this information.

Make the Estimated Payments

As a new business owner, you probably know how important it is for you to pay your taxes accurately and on time. However, many self-employed persons are also responsible for making estimated tax payments each quarter through the year.

During your first year of operation, you are excused from making these estimated tax payments. However, you are still responsible for doing it in the second year and onwards. Business owners who file as sole proprietors or a partner in the S-corporation must all start making estimated tax payments any time they anticipate that they will owe $1,000 or more for that tax year.

You Must Pay the Self-Employment Tax

For those who are brand new to owning a business, you may not be sure what the self-employment tax is all about. This tax is comprised of the Medicare and Social Security taxes, and it is owed by anyone who doesn't have employer withholding on them. Since you are self-employed and don't have your own employer any longer, you will be responsible for both your own portion and the portion that is usually paid by an employer to satisfy this tax.

To help ease their burden a little bit when it comes to tax time, you should try to deduct the employer-equivalent component of their self-employment tax. Doing this, and making sure that you claim all the right deductions will ensure that you are able to keep this tax as low as possible at the end of the year.

Tax Deductions for Your Small Business

If you are new to running a small business, you may not know all the expenses that you are able to deduct when it comes to tax time. Taking advantage of these deductions can make a big difference in how much your tax bill will be when tax season comes. Some of the best tax deductions that your small business should check out include the following:

- Vehicle expenses: Many small businesses use a vehicle to help them out. Operating that vehicle and the costs of it, for your business is deductible. But you must have proof and records that you used that vehicle for business.

- Wages and salaries: The payments that you make to employees, including their wages, salaries, commissions, bonuses, and some taxable fringe benefits can be deducted from your expenses.

- Contract labor: Many small businesses are going to use independent contractors or freelancers to help them meet their labor needs. The cost of this contract labor can be deductible. If you are doing this, you need to issue a Form 1099-MISC to any contractor that receives $600 or more from you in that year. If you send them their payment through PayPal or credit card, then these companies will issue them a 1099-K, but it is still a good idea to send out the form for your own protection.

- Supplies: The cost of items that you purchased to run your business can be deductible. They need to be used specifically for the business, or you can't deduct them.

- Rent on your business property: If you rented out a space to conduct business in, then you can deduct this amount.

- Utilities: The electricity that you pay for the facility can be deductible. You can also deduct phone costs if it is used just for the business.

- Insurance: If you use insurance in your business, such as a business owner's policy or malpractice coverage, then you can deduct it at tax time. There are some rules when it comes to deducting health insurance though. A small business may qualify to claim a tax credit for a maximum of 50 percent of the premiums paid for employees, which is a better break than the deduction.

- Travel: If you or someone on your team travels to conduct the business, the cost of transportation and the lodging for that person is deductible. There are some exceptions to this. For example, commuting locally to work or to see clients is not going to count under this deduction.

- Advertising: Any of the ordinary costs of advertising your business can be deductible.

- Home office: A portion of your personal expenses for a home office is deductible during tax time if you use it for your business. If you conduct any business there, such as working on reports, meeting with clients and so on, then you can deduct some of these things for your taxes.

- Legal and professional fees: Anything that you pay for accounting or legal fees are fully deductible.

- Meals and entertainment: These costs can be deducted, but only up to 50 percent. So if you take a client out to lunch to work on the business, half of it will be covered by taxes. The meal has to be used for business purposes or to further your business. You can't decide to take a break from work and count that unless you are actually conducting business during that lunch.

- Interest on any of your debts for the business: Any of the interest you pay on loans can be deductible. Starting in 2018, businesses that have the average annual gross receipts for the three prior years of over $25 million will be limited in the percentage of interest that you can deduct. And any interest on a personal loan that was used to help the business will be treated as well.

- Any employee benefit programs: The costs that you incur for any of the benefit programs you offer your employees, such as retirement plans, dependent care assistance, and education assistance, can be deductible. For someone who is self-employed, the contributions to their own retirement plans, the ones that are qualified, can be a personal deduction.

- Mortgage interest: A business that own realty is able to take the mortgage interest they play and fully deduct it.

Claiming all the business expenses that you have will do wonders to helping you limit the amount that you need to pay during tax time. You can work with your accountant to figure out which of these, and other deductions, you can use to assist you in keeping more money in your pocket during tax time.

How to Prepare W2s for Your Employees

If you have employees, you will need to know how to prepare a W2. When you hire a new employee, you need to ask them to fill out a W4 for a regular employee, or a W9 for an independent contractor. You will need this information to help you prepare your W2s.

The W4 form needs to be on file with the business the whole time that the employee works with you. If there are changes that you need to make to this file, such as when an employee moves, then you need to have them fill out a new form. Before preparing the W2, make sure that all your employees take a look at their W4 to ensure that the information is up to date and accurate.

You will need to get all the information that the W2 requires. This will include the social security number of the employee (so it matches up when they do taxes), their name, address, how much they made and so on. Once you have all this information, you can then review and create your W2s.

Any employee who works for you at some point during the year will need to get a W2 from your business. It doesn't matter if they only worked for a few months or if they quit at the beginning of the year, or anything else. If they worked even one day for you during that fiscal year, then they need to get a W2.

There are various methods that you can use to get the W2 forms ready for printing. You can get them directly from the IRS, use a tax or accounting software, ask your CPA, or even purchase them from a local office supply store. When it comes to getting them from the IRS website, you are not able to directly download it from the site.

If you have the capabilities of doing this, an accounting software that has a payroll feature can help. You can just add this on, and the work will be done with you. The accounting software can keep track of all the information for the year and then you just need to go through it and ensure the information is accurate before you print it off.

Next, you need to distribute the W2s so that your employees are able to use them on their own tax returns. You must get these to your employees by January 31 at the latest. You can send out these out through the mail, or you can have your employees pick them up. Some businesses are also choosing to have these documents available on a secured website to make it easier on everyone and to ensure that all the employees have a copy, won't lose it, and will get the information in time.

Once the employees all have their W2s, it is time to figure out how you are going to file them with the Social Security Administration. You need to file form W-3 complete with a copy A of each W2 for your employees. Two other methods you can use to file these forms include the following:

- File online through the business services online section of the Social Security website. You will need to go through some registration steps to file this electronically.

- Mail completed forms of W2 and W3 to the Social Security Administration.

If you are in a state where the employee needs to pay their state taxes, then copy 1 of the W2 needs to be sent to the state taxing authority for each state that the employee worked in and paid taxes to.

A huge part of bookkeeping is preparing the books for tax season. That is why, as a bonus, I am adding this chapter about taxes for small businesses.

If you are just starting, you may feel overwhelmed at tax time. You should not need to feel this way. As long as you keep your records up-to-date, it should be a breeze when it comes time for taxes.

When it comes to tax deductions for running your small business, there are so many to think about. I compiled a list of some other types of deductions for you to consider.

- Employees' pay—this can be deducted as long as the pay is in the form of cash, property, or services.

- Inventory (cost of goods sold)—if your business manufacture products or purchases products for resale you can deduct the cost of goods sold.

- Employee benefits—such benefits like healthcare, adoption assistance, education assistance, and life insurance can be deducted.

- Home office—make sure you have a dedicated room for your home office. You will need to calculate the square footage so that you can apply a percentage of your rent, mortgage, insurance, utilities, housekeeping, etc. That percentage can be deducted if you work out of your home.

- Auto maintenance and mileage—there are two ways to calculate this rate. You can use the standard mileage rate or the actual expenses paid. Be sure to use whichever gives you the greatest deduction.

- Advertising and marketing—you can deduct the cost of marketing and advertising your business. This includes promotion costs for good publicity.

- Office supplies—this can be anything you use for your office. Make sure you keep your receipt of all items. These are small day-to-day items.

- Education—this includes educating people about your business through seminars and trade shows. Also, if you have magazines, books, CD's and DVD's that relate to your business, they are 100% deductible.

- Professional fees—this includes accountant, lawyer and consulting fees. They are 100% deductible.

- Travel expenses—when the travel is business related it is mostly all 100% deductible. This includes airfare, hotels, and other road expenses. However, eating out can be deducted but only at 50%.

- Entertainment—this one can be tricky. If you are just going out with coworkers, it is not deductible. However, if you bring a client or prospective client, you can deduct 50%. Same goes for if you take them out for drinks as long as it is in a business setting or business meeting.

- Furniture—this is supposed to have a long lifespan. Therefore, you can deduct the full cost of the furniture at one time, or you can deduct the depreciation over several years.

- Office equipment—this will be those big items such a fax machine, copier, or computer. They are also 100% deductible and can be deducted the same way as the furniture.

- Employee or client gifts—it is always nice to reward your employees or clients with a gift. These are 100% deductible up to $25 per year for each person.

- Startup expenses (capital expenses)—you can deduct up to $5,000. This includes research costs that you incurred for creating your business.

- Taxes—that's right. Taxes that incurred through running your business can be deductible.

- Insurance premiums—the credit, liability, malpractice, and workers' compensation premiums call all be deducted.

- Interest—the interest that you incur from mortgage, finance charges such as credit cards, payment plans, and interest on loans are 100% deductible.

- Software—this includes boxed, downloadable, and subscriptions. They are all deductible.

- Charitable contributions—if the contribution is more than $250 you will need a letter from the organization verifying the contribution. If the donation is not money, you can visit the IRS website and look up Publication 561: Determining the Value of Donated Property.

- Rent—if you rent and the property is used for your business you can deduct the rent. However, if you receive any of that rent as equity, you are not able to deduct it.

- Freelancers—when you hire an independent contractor you can deduct their pay as a business expense.

- Repairs and maintenance—when you run a business there will always be some repairs and maintenance needed to be done for your business to run smoothly still. These are deductible.

- Licenses—license fees and regulatory fees are deductible.

- There are so many more. With a little research, you could find deductions that you never knew existed.

Bookkeeping Tips
for Your Small Business

The Best Bookkeeping Tips for Your Business

As a new entrepreneur, you have a lot of financial details that you have to keep track of to help the business run efficiently. Doing this well has a lot of advantages. It can help you to make sure that you are making profits and understand exactly where your money is going each month. It helps you to be prepared for tax season at the end of the year. And it can ensure that you are paying your employees properly and that your business is growing the way that you want.

Getting started with bookkeeping may seem a bit confusing when you first get started. There are many different forms that you need to pay attention to, and this can be scary for a lot of beginners who have never experienced these before. Let's look at some of the best bookkeeping tips that you can follow to help your business stay financially secure.

Plan for the Major Expenses

There are times when a big expense is going to come up. If you don't plan for these issues, you will either put yourself in trouble with money, miss out on some big opportunities, or have to go out with something. When you plan for these major expenses, and they are going to show up at some point, you will either have to miss out on a business opportunity that is important to you, or you may have to scramble for a loan from the bank if you have to pay. For example, if your computer system crashes and you need to pay for some IT to come in, it is much better to have this money on hand rather than scrambling to get a loan and get it fixed in time.

There are several things that you can do when this happens. First, put some big events, like a computer upgrade that is needed, on the calendar a year in advance. If you can, write this down every year for the next three to five years. You can also acknowledge on the calendar some of the seasonal ups and downs the business has and make sure that you are putting enough money aside to make it through these leaner months as well.

Often the costly things that you need to fix are going to show up in the slower months for your company. Do you really want to get caught in the trap of taking out money during the busy periods, just to find out that you are short on money for major repairs in some of the slower months?

Track All the Expenses

You want to keep accurate records of all the expenses and transactions that come up with your business. Tracking these not only give you a good idea on how the finances of the business are doing, but it can help you with tax season. If you don't keep good track of the expenses that you take on during the year, you might miss some tax write-offs or have to give up on a few because you just don't have the right information.

Having the right bookkeeping methods in place, and keeping all the receipts of your business along the way, can help you out here. You should either have everything added and uploaded to your online bookkeeping software or have another system of accounting that you can work with to help keep everything organized. This will go a long way in helping you see results.

This means that you should keep track of everything that you do with your business and every expense that you take for the business. This includes any events that take cash, any coffee dates, lunches, and business trips, should be kept track of. This habit is going to go a long way toward substantiating those items for your tax records in case you are audited. These records make sure that you are safe in case the IRS wants to look at your records and can make it easier to know what tax deductions you get in the first place.

Record the Deposits Correctly

The reason that this one is so important is that it makes it less likely that you are going to pay taxes on money that isn't income. You never want to pay more taxes than you need to, especially when it comes to paying it on money that isn't your income.

The best thing here is to take up a system that will keep all the financial activities of your business straight, whether it is a notebook that you use on a regular basis, the help of an Excel spreadsheet, or some software that can record all your financial information.

Being a business owner, you need to make a wide variety of deposits into your bank account throughout a fiscal year, including deposits about revenue from any sales, cash infusions from the personal savings, or loans. The trouble here is that when the year ends, you (or a bookkeeping you decide to work with), might go through this information and then record some of the deposits as income when they aren't your income. And when this happens, you could end up paying taxes on more money than what you actually made that year.

Set Money for Your Taxes

If you are past the first year of business, or you are a sole proprietorship who owed the IRS $1,000 or more for a year, then you need to file quarterly tax returns. If you fail to do this, then the IRS could levy interest and penalties for not filing these on time.

The best thing to do is to systematically put some of the money aside during the year that you can use to pay your taxes. Then, on the calendar, you will note the deadlines for the taxes, along with any preparation time if it is needed. This ensures that you are actually able to make the tax payments to the IRS on time when they are due.

One thing that can be especially problematic for your business is payroll taxes. There are times when some entrepreneurs, who aren't taking care of their finances properly, will be crash-crunched and end up in a down cycle. They will dip into the employee withholdings, the money that was earmarked to be sent to the IRS.

If you start messing with these payroll taxes, you are going to end up with a twofold problem. First, you haven't paid the taxes that are due for the employees, and you have taken money that the IRS sees as belonging to the employees. The IRS is not going to be very happy about this situation, and you will end up in a lot of trouble. Set aside some money to help you pay your quarterly taxes.

Keep a Tab on the Invoices That You Have

You will quickly find in your business that any late bills or unpaid bills are going to cut into the cash flow that you have. When people are not paying the invoice that they owe to you, and you had to pay for employees to do the work and materials, this can really end up putting you behind. You had to pay for everything upfront, and now you have to make due and keep getting things paid upfront for other customers, without having that money from the original customers.

You have to always keep track of the invoices that you have to make sure they are all paid on time. It is important to designate someone in your company to keep track of your billing. Then put a process in place so that you can make phone calls, send out a second invoice, and levying penalties, such as extra fees at a certain deadline.

When it comes to the invoices that you have, you want to make sure that you have a plan in the event one of your customers doesn't pay their bill to you yet, since this can influence the cash flow so much. Come up with a plan of what you will need to do if the customer is thirty, sixty, or ninety days late on an invoice that you sent them.

Don't fall into the trap of thinking that once you sent out an invoice to a customer, that your billing is taken care of. Every late payment is basically an interest-free loan, and it is going to seriously harm the cash flow of your business. You want to keep sending out invoices and have a good plan in place to ensure that you are getting the message out to your customer and that they will pay for the product or service.

Conclusion

This book has given you the tools to better understand not only your bookkeeper but your business as well. These are all areas that you, as a business owner, need to know and understand.

Each area that we have covered has a purpose. When you work hand-in-hand with your bookkeeper, you will see the light at the end of the tunnel.

I mentioned in the beginning, "It is not the business owner that runs the business. It is the business owner teamed up with the bookkeeper that truly runs the business."

I want to take a minute to break down that statement. As the business owner, you have the power to make the decisions that will move your business forward. Your business will succeed or fail based on your decisions.

Your bookkeeper is the gatekeeper. They hold power over the financial health of your business. With their mighty power, you can have all the financial statements you need when you need them. They can also ensure that all the transactions are correct.

As a team, you are unstoppable. Your bookkeeper can ensure you have what is needed to move your business in the right direction. They can also help guide you in making the right decisions. With the proper analysis and ratios, you can predict the future if the trend is steady.

Now I have empowered you to be on the same level as your bookkeeper and accountant.

If you have not started your business yet but you are thinking about it and currently doing the research for your business, then this is a great place to start.

With the knowledge that you have learned, you will also be better prepared to add your financials to your business plan and pitch deck.

Best of luck to all your endeavors. I look forward to seeing your business up and running and hearing about the great success you will be having.